GAMBLE ROGERS

UNIVERSITY PRESS OF FLORIDA

Florida A&M University, Tallahassee
Florida Atlantic University, Boca Raton
Florida Gulf Coast University, Ft. Myers
Florida International University, Miami
Florida State University, Tallahassee
New College of Florida, Sarasota
University of Central Florida, Orlando
University of Florida, Gainesville
University of North Florida, Jacksonville
University of South Florida, Tampa
University of West Florida, Pensacola

University Press of Florida
Gainesville · Tallahassee · Tampa · Boca Raton
Pensacola · Orlando · Miami · Jacksonville · Ft. Myers · Sarasota

Gamble Rogers

A Troubadour's Life

Bruce Horovitz

Title page: Gamble Rogers on Conch Island in St. Augustine. Photo by Bob Patterson.

Library of Congress Control Number: 2017957464
ISBN 978-0-8130-5694-4

The University Press of Florida is the scholarly publishing agency for the State University System of Florida, comprising Florida A&M University, Florida Atlantic University, Florida Gulf Coast University, Florida International University, Florida State University, New College of Florida, University of Central Florida, University of Florida, University of North Florida, University of South Florida, and University of West Florida.

University Press of Florida
15 Northwest 15th Street
Gainesville, FL 32611-2079
http://upress.ufl.edu

In memory of my parents, Roz and Elliott,
may their names be for a blessing.

Contents

Author's Note

The idea for this book came from discussions with several of Gamble Rogers's closest friends. Most of the material in the book was derived from more than forty interviews with members of Gamble Rogers's family and his musician friends, professional associates, and personal acquaintances. Every interview was conducted with the understanding that the material gathered was for the exclusive use in this book about Gamble Rogers's life. The author would like to acknowledge and express appreciation to all of them and extend special thanks to Gamble Rogers's longtime friend and agent-manager, Charles V. Steadham Jr., founding director of the Gamble Rogers Memorial Foundation.

In addition to the interviews, the author relied on recordings and documents at the foundation website, GambleRogers.com, and held in the State Library and Archives of Florida, as well as works of Gamble Rogers and others published elsewhere. These sources are cited in the notes, discography, and appendixes and have been quoted for the purposes of criticism and review. Excerpts are reproduced with permission where required.

Prologue

THE TATTERED FLAG FLYING LIMP over the Terminal Tavern was at half-staff. It was so ordered by Agamemnon Jones, chief philosopher at Erindale's Purina Store, where Oklawaha County's metaphysicians would gather at the loading ramp to preach the aphorisms of the day to anybody who would listen.

The Reverend Jeremiah Proudfoot of the Bean Creek Baptist Church had proclaimed it the "Sorriest Day for the Sorriest County in All of Florida."

The dirt parking lot of the Terminal Tavern on Redbug Road between Snipes Ford and Bean Creek was filled to capacity with an acre and a half of pickup trucks. Sheriff Hutto Proudfoot, the preacher's son, was there handling security.

Shelby III, Hylo Poindexter, Downwind Dave, and eight others arrived in their shackle block Chevrolet, a car so sorry you had to go sixty miles an hour just to get the headlights to come on. The county's rabbi, Bubba, arrived shortly thereafter.

Oklawaha County's symbol for sorriness, Still Bill, was there along with his wife, War Bunny, and their three-legged Chihuahua, aptly named Flat Tire.

Even the Hell's Belles, the intrepid good ol' girls motorcycle gang, had come to the Terminal Tavern on this darkest of days riding their dirt bikes and wearing wet suits with sleeveless Villager shirts and earrings attached by staple guns.

Chester the Molester and Forklift Mary arrived by Airstream trailer to join other members of the William Faulkner Literary Society, lovers of literature, each and every one.

They had all assembled at this dank, cavernous temple of culture known as the Terminal Tavern for a single purpose: to mourn one of their own.

Gamble Rogers, the acclaimed Troubadour Emeritus of Oklawaha County, had passed on. Rogers had attained this lofty title by having performed for twenty consecutive years as the house act at the Terminal Tavern.

The folk singing troubadour had given these noble residents a voice and a sense of their own worth by teaching them that sorriness was a virtue. "Sorry is as sorry does," he would remind them.

In his twenty years as the house bard, he poked fun at every one of them, often reciting words so big they would have looked them up in the dictionary if they'd only had an alphabet. He used his humor to make a point about life, society, and the perils of progress. He never degraded a single one of them. In fact, more often than not he had them laughing at themselves.

On this solemn day of mourning, Reverend Proudfoot announced to the rakish gathering that there would be no eulogy for the Troubadour Emeritus of Oklawaha County, only a moment of silence. In the midst of the deafening quiet, Elfrieda, the exotic dancer, moseyed on over to the tavern's Wurlitzer jukebox and played the mellifluous tones of Miss Peggy Lee singing that grand old American standard "Fever."

Somewhere, up in heaven, Gamble Rogers was smiling, remembering an important lesson he learned himself from Agamemnon Jones—"When your work speaks for itself, don't interrupt."

Introduction

IT WAS IN THE EARLY EVENING HOURS of October 10, 1991, when the phone rang inside the residential trailer nestled in the woods off Rattlesnake Road in Lake Wales, Florida.

"We've lost Gamble," uttered the subdued voice of the caller.

"Lost him? Well you better go find him."

The news was so stunning it never even registered. Gamble Rogers, Florida's beloved troubadour, was lost forever. How could it be that this legendary figure, bigger than life, could be gone in an instant? All of the mystique, the charisma, the charm, and the downright goodness washed away without even the slightest warning.

To those who knew him, Gamble Rogers's sudden, tragic death was the ultimate paradox. It came as no surprise that he took it upon himself to strip to his shirt and underwear, blow up an air mattress, and try to rescue a perfect stranger from the fierce nor'easter wreaking havoc on the Florida coast. However, it was obvious that the creator of a treasured repository of Florida folklore had no chance. At age fifty-four, his mobility was limited by an arthritic back condition discovered in adolescence that plagued him most of his life. "He couldn't swim in a swimming pool, much less the ocean," remarked a close friend.

While there was no autopsy, the cause of death seemed far less important than the "Good Causes" he left behind, the title track from a CD released after his death. The fact that Florida even has a folk tradition was due in large measure to Gamble Rogers and the community of mythical misfits and malcontents he imagined and brought to life night after night in remote pubs and taverns across the state. His followers would return to hear the very same stories over and over, looking for a new nuance or simply because they just needed another good laugh. More than a polished performer and storyteller, Gamble connected with people regardless of their backgrounds or status.

"He could relate to a fruit picker with no education just as easily as he could the president of the United States," said a contemporary. In typical fashion, when he arrived at a party he would make sure to greet the kids and the dogs first, before mingling with his admirers and well wishers, recalled his close pal and fellow folksinger Bob Patterson.

"In the final analysis," Gamble often quipped, "the size of one's funeral is always determined by the weather." Not so in his case. A single memorial service wouldn't suffice. There would be three separate public gatherings in Florida within days of his death. Tributes poured in from across the country, from Pete Seeger, Jimmy Buffett, Tom Paxton. "Gamble was the greatest spirit I've ever known. I loved him," wrote Paxton. Strangers weighed in with stories of how meeting Gamble changed their lives.

Lost at sea in the Florida surf would be so many lasting images: the distinctive chin, the corkscrew gait, the onstage facial contortions, and the sight of his faded, lime green 1965 fastback Mustang parked outside a local saloon signaling that Gamble was in town.

A persona consultant could not have come up with a better name, such that the last name Rogers almost became superfluous. It was just "Gamble this" and "Gamble that."

He had a look that fit the part. "You could have put his face as the marquee of the labor movement or the folk movement," recalled St. Augustine folksinger Charlie Robertson. "He just had that chiseled look of something out of 'Let Us Now Praise Famous Men.' It was a look that defined America."

As it turns out, the mission to find Gamble Rogers was easier said than done. For certain, his physical body, belly distended, was brought ashore on Flagler Beach only moments after his heroic but fatal attempt to rescue a drowning Canadian tourist. But there was so much more.

Finding the real Gamble Rogers, the man behind the myth, was a much bigger challenge. Who was this man, so revered that a quarter century after his untimely death, the mere mention of his name brings tears to the eyes of so many he befriended? Who was this folksinging raconteur who shed the family's well-to-do upbringing and architecture pedigree for a life on the road performing in honky-tonks and college campuses from Florida to California and all places in between, including a gig with the legendary Doc Watson at Carnegie Hall?

How is it that the folklorist often compared to Mark Twain and Will Rogers has remained an enigma? Even in his home state of Florida, where an annual music festival, middle school, and state park bear his name, he is a fading memory. Despite having been inducted into the Florida Artists Hall of Fame with cultural icons like Ernest Hemingway, Marjorie Kinnan Rawlings, and Tennessee Williams, Gamble Rogers remains a virtual unknown to those outside his orbit.

There have even been politicized efforts to have his name removed from the state park dedicated to his memory. One city official told the *St. Augustine Record* newspaper, "No one really knew who he was." The official reasoned that changing the park's name back to the original Flagler Beach State Recreation Area would attract more tourists and improve the economy.

"What a crass tradeoff for the life of a legend," responded the *St. Augustine Record* on its editorial page. Legend indeed. While he never had a record on the hit parade, Gamble assembled an intensely dedicated, cultlike following of admirers and proteges.

"Everyone wanted to play guitar like Gamble," said a fellow folk musician. "But more than that, everyone wanted to be like Gamble." His life has been memorialized in dozens of tribute ballads and folksongs, some written by performers who never knew him but were inspired by his spirit.

A chance encounter with one of his earliest childhood friends started my own search to find Gamble Rogers. Despite having lived right in the middle of Gamble's prime years and in close proximity to his performing neighborhood, I too missed out on one of the most prolific and charismatic figures to emerge from the 1960s folk culture.

Believing it's never too late, I began my search to find Gamble Rogers. His life was a journey of Americana in its truest sense. It began on the intimate Isle of Sicily in Winter Park, Florida, and wound its way up to the hills of the Nacoochee Valley in northeastern Georgia, where Gamble spent his formative summers working on the family farm while spying on the Sky Lake Campfire Girls. Here was the imagery that laid the foundation for his Southern Gothic tales and helped populate the landscape of his fictitious Oklawaha County.

In my search I retraced seminal moments in Gamble's life, from his meeting with William Faulkner at the University of Virginia to his unscheduled stop in Greenwich Village, where a last-minute audition with the Serendipity Singers would solidify his folksinging career, forever ending his brief flirtation with the family's prestigious architecture legacy. Serendipity indeed! Gamble was on the way to seek work with an architecture firm in Massachusetts when he took the detour that would change his life forever.

It was a journey back in time to a bygone era that produced a generation of black sheep who would seek their own means of creativity and expression to change the world rather than pursue preordained family destinies. I encountered colorful characters, some real and some not, and some of the most flavorful taverns of the era, like St. Augustine's notorious Tradewinds Tropical Lounge, Chicago's Earl of Old Town, and the now defunct Flick coffeehouse in Coconut Grove, Florida, that hosted, among others, a young Joni Mitchell and the folk goddess Odetta.

Most of all Gamble's life embodied the human spirit, filled with triumph and tragedy. The sound track of his career was a smooth but purposeful arrangement of unforgettable choke-style guitar picking laced with uproarious yet often poignant polysyllable storytelling with a bullseye aimed squarely at life's many ironies.

In the end, my journey to find Gamble Rogers was a search for the truth. But as with so many folk legends, the real truth is often obscured. It should come as no surprise that there are conflicting versions of the story.

So, who was the real Gamble Rogers? Was it the guitar picker extraordinaire who, along with Will McLean, Jim Ballew, and Paul Champion ushered in a renaissance of Florida folk music in the mid-1970s through the early 1980s?

Was it Gamble Rogers the linguistic humorist, who preached the erudite philosophies of Still Bill, Agamemnon Jones, War Bunny,

Downwind Dave, and other rural alchemists who inhabited the primitive backwoods squalor of Oklawaha County and held court at the Terminal Tavern?

Was it Gamble Rogers the family man, who balanced the demands of a hectic professional life with that of being a devoted father and a friend to those who loved and knew him best?

Was it Gamble Rogers the environmentalist, who sought peace and inspiration traversing Florida's natural waters and parks with his trusty kayak and battered bicycle?

Or was it Gamble Rogers the giving soul, who thought not for a minute before making the ultimate sacrifice of plunging into the raging sea to save a perfect stranger?

Maybe Gamble himself answered it best. When interviewed for the radio show *The Songs of Florida* he was asked, "What do you consider yourself to be, a guitar player, a humorist, a storyteller, or a folksinger?" Gamble replied, "Well, I ain't nothing more than a whiskey salesman. I play in these dives and the more whiskey they drink, the more money I make."

The search to find Gamble Rogers has its historical roots near the end of the Revolutionary War in the stockades at Bryan Station, Kentucky, with none other than Daniel Boone.

I

My Father
Was a Voyager

1

JOSEPH HALE ROGERS, born in 1742, was living on a fifty-acre farm in Culpepper, Virginia, when he was approached by a neighbor, William Preston, then the surveyor of Fincastle County, about a land swap. It seems Preston wanted to expand his own farm and offered Rogers a trade, deed for deed, for a parcel of land outside of Lexington, Kentucky, in a place called Bryan Station. The deal was done, sight unseen. It was one of several land deals that would play a definitive role in the life of the Rogers family.

Bryan Station was a fortified settlement that was the scene of a significant battle siege near the end of the American Revolutionary War when, on August 15, 1782, it was attacked by Shawnee Indians and British Canadians.

According to a Rogers family history, Joseph Hale Rogers and his brother arrived in Bryan Station about a year prior to the siege, prospecting for a home: "For that reason, they were there at the time of the siege and fought there."

Family talk has it that Joseph Hale Rogers ended up in the stockades along with Daniel Boone, who is believed to have lost one of his sons, Israel Boone, in the nearby bloody Battle of Blue Licks that ensued only a few days after the siege of Bryan Station. Joseph Hale Rogers survived the encounter.

Descendants of the Rogers family remained in Bryan Station, where the renowned architect James Gamble Rogers I was born in 1867. He was the first in the family to be known as Gamble and the first in a lineage of prestigious American architects that would span beyond the next century. Among his most notable works was a series of buildings he designed for his alma mater, Yale University, including the Harkness Memorial Quadrangle, the Sterling Library, and the Sterling Law School. Other projects included designs for Sophie Newcomb College in New Orleans and the Columbia-Presbyterian Medical Center.

His brother John Arthur Rogers was born in Kentucky in 1870. After the Great Chicago Fire of 1871, the family moved to that city in search of better economic opportunities. Like his older brother, John Arthur Rogers pursued a career in architecture. The two practiced together intermittently.

At age forty-three, John Arthur Rogers, in the midst of a distinguished architecture career, suffered a serious heart attack and was told he had a short time to live. His doctor advised him to move to a warmer climate for his health. In 1915 John Arthur Rogers loaded his family into a Model T Ford and made the arduous two-week trek from Illinois to Florida, where they settled in Daytona Beach.

By the time they arrived in Daytona, John Arthur's son, James Gamble Rogers II, was a teenager. He was already showing signs of immense talent when he enrolled as a junior at Daytona's Seabreeze High School. The next in the family to be known as Gamble, he excelled in athletics, showed a proclivity for writing, and was already becoming a talented musician specializing in the tenor banjo and the piano.

His first attempt to attend Dartmouth College was put on hold, in part because the college had never heard of his high school and wanted proof of the school's accreditation. Undeterred, he took a job at Daytona Merchants Bank before finally receiving a swimming scholarship to Dartmouth in 1921. With the money he earned at the bank, Gamble II purchased a Vega longneck tenor banjo for $175, a little less than half the cost of an automobile in 1920.

At Dartmouth, Gamble II set the intercollegiate time record for the 100-yard breast stroke and qualified for the 1924 Olympic swim team. (The 1924 Olympics would be the setting for the blockbuster movie *Chariots of Fire*, released in 1981.)

In addition to athletics and academics, Gamble II pursued his musical interests at Dartmouth, forming a band known as the Midnight

Sons in which he played tenor banjo and an occasional novelty number on the piano.

It was at Dartmouth that he attended a performance by John "Sleepy" Hall, an accomplished tenor banjo player from Yale who would later tour and record with Rudy Vallee and the band Sleepy Hall and His Collegians. On this particular evening, a big-band orchestra was playing in the gymnasium when Sleepy Hall entered the center of the dance floor with a tenor banjo in one hand and a drafting stool in the other. Hall crawled up on the stool and started playing his banjo over the sounds of the big band on stage. Everyone stopped dancing and formed a circle around the charismatic banjo picker. Within minutes Sleepy Hall, playing a lone tenor banjo, shut down the big band and took over the room. The moment was not lost on Gamble II, who would retell the story to his own family many years later.

Gamble II's love of music and appreciation for the creativity of playing a stringed instrument would stay with him throughout his adult life. It would provide him with some measure of understanding later in life when his own son wanted to play the guitar for a living rather than pursue a more traditional life.

While en route to the 1924 Paris Olympics, Gamble II received an urgent message that his father, John Arthur, who had maintained a modest architecture practice in Daytona, had suffered a second serious heart attack. Dreams of the Olympics and a degree from Dartmouth were cut short. There was a family business to run. Despite having no formal training in architecture, Gamble II was on his way back to Florida, where he was destined to become one the state's preeminent architects of the twentieth century and father to a legendary guitar-picking "whiskey salesman."

2

ONCE BACK IN DAYTONA, James Gamble Rogers II began what amounted to a ten-year apprenticeship under his father's direction, moving quickly from draftsman to building designer. Since he was not a licensed architect, his work needed to be signed by his father or one of the other architects in the firm. Nevertheless, Gamble II proved more than adept at learning the family trade, and his artistic talent was emerging by the time he opened a branch office in the town of Winter Park, Florida, in 1928.

He was also about to meet the love of his life. At a beach party in Daytona, Gamble II found himself coming to the aid of an attractive redhead seeking refuge from her date, who had indulged in a few too many drinks.

Evelyn Claire Smith was the oldest of five children. Despite having only a year of college at Agnes Scott College in Decatur, Georgia, Evelyn was a voracious reader. She was bright and decidedly Old South, with long, auburn hair almost down to her waist. Her father was an entrepreneur who worked briefly at the *Atlanta Constitution* at the same time as did the journalist and folklorist Joel Chandler Harris, author of the Uncle Remus and Br'er Rabbit tales. As a result, Evelyn grew up reading Uncle Remus and perfected the dialect. In later years she would sometimes read aloud from the books when hosting parties in Winter Park for English professors at Rollins College or an occasional visiting professor from Oxford or Cambridge.

As she sought to distance herself from her tipsy date in Daytona that evening, she found the young architecture apprentice, who was attending the party alone, and together they agreed to take a walk on the beach. On the way they picked up a bottle of olives. A courtship ensued, and the two were married in 1929. A bottle of olives became the traditional anniversary gift during their sixty years of marriage.

Shortly after their wedding, Gamble II secured a lot on the undeveloped Isle of Sicily on Lake Maitland in Winter Park. There he designed and built their residence, a French provincial cottage known as Four Winds. The house was recognized in several architectural magazines and offered further evidence that Gamble Rogers II was beginning to attract local and national attention.

He still needed an architecture license. Having served sufficient time as an apprentice and with some significant work under his belt, Gamble II sat for the state's licensing exam in 1934. He failed. His exam project was a hotel, which he designed around a big, central atrium. The architects on the review panel told him the design was the most impractical thing they had ever seen and flunked him. He retook the exam in 1935 and passed.

It was time to build his practice and his family, but not before a brush with death during the Great Hurricane of 1938 aboard the yacht *Caprice* during its shakedown cruise from Fort Lauderdale to Jacksonville. Gamble II agreed to join the crew of the *Caprice*'s new owners, who had bought the fifty-five-foot, gaff-rigged ketch secondhand in Fort Lauderdale.

It was before the days of the more sophisticated hurricane warning systems, so the crew was dependent on local radar. "Fair weather with moderate to fresh east winds" was the thirty-six-hour forecast. In an unpublished essay, Gamble II chronicled the nightmare journey as the massive hurricane traveled up the East Coast.

We realized the absolute necessity of preventing the sea from breaking over the ketch, for it was doubtful that any boat, no matter how stoutly built could stand this sort of beating without breaking up. . . . During the night the hurricane became more terrifying, the wind rising to such a pitch it literally screamed through the rigging. . . . Darkness was absolute and complete, not even the silhouette of a spar against the sky being visible. Sleep was impossible. The noise was deafening and even though one's ears had long since become numbed from the constant roar, we couldn't help listening for some new sound which might presage a failure in Caprice's structure . . . Time dragged through that awful night, each new morning more eagerly sought.

Gamble II and the crew miraculously survived the mighty storm, which turned north before wreaking massive destruction and devastation in New England.

Back home on the Isle of Sicily in Winter Park, there awaited Gamble II's wife, Evelyn, who was expecting, and their eighteen-month-old son, James Gamble Rogers IV.

II

Tales of a
Misspent Youth

3

Bruce McEwan loves to ask a trick question. The retired attorney and former state legislator from Orlando, with a cigar in hand, pulls out a slightly wrinkled black and white photograph of two babies in diapers and asks, "Want to guess who this is?"

To the uninitiated the photograph seems innocuous enough. But to McEwan, it's a treasured artifact that's a gateway to a historic and deeply personal past. "That's Gamble Rogers and me . . . only back then he was Jimmy."

Long before he was to establish himself as Florida's troubadour, James Gamble Rogers IV was simply known as Jimmy. (The name James Gamble Rogers III was given to the grandson of James Gamble Rogers I.)

Bruce McEwan was Jimmy's first friend. They shared a lot more than the early photograph. McEwan's father was the physician who delivered Jimmy Rogers on January 31, 1937, and Jimmy's father, Gamble II, was the architect who designed the McEwan family home in Orlando.

"I guess it was pretty well assumed when we were kids that Jimmy would be an architect just like his father and I would be a physician just like my dad," McEwan said. "That's just what you did back then."

Fate and circumstances would dictate something very different. The two would remain good friends until the tragic ending at the Flagler Beach state park. Fifty-five years after they were photographed together in diapers, McEwan had the bittersweet role of cosponsoring legislation to rename the park in memory of his lifelong friend.

"He was a gentleman and a gentle man," said McEwan.

Bruce McEwan may have been Jimmy's first friend, but no one knew him better or spent more time with Jimmy growing up than his own brother Jack. John Hopewell Rogers was born on December 17, 1938. Known as Jack, he and Jimmy shared a room before they attended college at the University of Virginia. Jack became a successful architect in his own right, working with the family firm in Winter Park until he retired.

It's been said if you want to know what Gamble Rogers sounded like, spend a few minutes talking with his brother, Jack. Their voices are nearly indistinguishable, as are their many physical similarities. Jack speaks in a comfortable but measured tone that exudes warmth. His smile is not forced. Like his folk singing brother, Jack seems to have an appreciation for life's ironies. He also likes to tell stories, especially when it comes to family stories.

Initially the two boys lived at Four Winds, the provincial cottage on the Isle of Sicily. In 1941 a seventeen-acre parcel known as Temple Grove became available in the heart of Winter Park. The property was so named because of the presence of the flavorful temple orange, a tangerine-orange cross that grew in the grove.

The boys' mother, Evelyn, took an immediate interest in the property. Her husband, now deeply ensconced in building his architecture practice, felt the property was well beyond the family's financial reach. He was, however, respectful of Evelyn's sheer will and determination.

Jack retells the story as told to him: "My father gave my mother permission to talk to the property's owner, Mrs. Dorsey, probably thinking that was the end of it. So, my mother went over and sat under the live oak tree that's still on the property and began the conversation by asking Mrs. Dorsey what she wanted."

The result was an arrangement by which the young Rogers family would move into the one-story house on Temple Grove in exchange for managing the orange trees, selling the fruit, and endorsing the checks over to Mrs. Dorsey until the property was paid for in full.

"Needless to say, my father was caught off guard by the whole arrangement," said Jack. The Four Winds home on the Isle of Sicily where they were now living had help launch Gamble II's architecture career. Now he was about to move into a little turn-of-the-century frame cottage with two bedrooms, a kitchen, a living room, and a screened-in porch. On the other hand, the property had a sizable orange grove in the middle of Winter Park, fronting Lake Osceola.

The family moved into the small house at Temple Grove, where they lived until 1948, when Gamble II built a larger, Greek Revival home on the property. He and Evelyn remained at Temple Grove for the rest of their lives.

Temple Grove is also where Jimmy and Jack Rogers were raised until they left for college. "As kids, we had a lot of freedom," recalled Jack. "By the time we were ten, we could be out on the lake independently. We could literally leave the house after breakfast and come back at suppertime."

Bruce McEwan remembered the nights he slept over at Jimmy's. "We had a lot more freedom at his house than I did at mine. We would sleep over in a room just off the main house with no parents telling us what we could and couldn't do. We were good boys, but you know . . ."

In spite of the freedom, the lines of demarcation were clear in the Rogers's home. Gamble II was completely focused on and dedicated to his architecture practice. When the events of World War II virtually shut down the construction industry, he temporarily suspended operations at his Winter Park office and opted for service with the Corps of Engineers, followed by a brief stint in Pensacola with Smith Shipyards, which was building tankers and landing craft for the military. When Gamble II reopened the office in Winter Park in 1945, his rapid ascension as a highly respected architect demanded his full attention. He was all nuts and bolts and completely focused on his professional life.

Evelyn was clearly the family matriarch. She created the home and orchestrated the various details of family life.

"She didn't mind much if Jimmy and I fought with each other," said Jack. "She just never wanted to come home to find out we were fighting on different sides. She was very much Old South, in that families were tight and they always held together."

While she was not in the family business, Evelyn Rogers was a lover of antiques and built her own reputation as an interior decorator, doing work in the Orlando Federal Savings and Loan building. Her family heritage was her love for land, an appreciation for proper furnishings, and her role as the heart of the family unit.

Meanwhile, Jimmy and Jack were as close as brothers could be. In lieu of an allowance the boys were allowed to pick oranges from the grove and sell them to local grocery stores.

"We were competitive until we were old enough to hurt each other," remembered Jack.

"Since we always shared a room, Jimmy and I had the opportunity to grow up together listening to the radio, at night, turning out the light, and seeing the images on the ceiling of what was on the radio."

Among the stations they listened to was Cincinnati's WCKY with its popular program *Country Music Jamboree*. There wasn't a television set in the Rogers family home at Temple Grove until the early 1970s.

"We were focused on reading, music, and storytelling," recalled Jack.

If there was a family interest beyond the growing architecture business, it was an appreciation for the great outdoors and a love of music. Like he did during his days at Dartmouth, Gamble II continued to play the piano and the tenor banjo for family and friends. He had developed an acute musical ear.

"He could hear someone in another room hit a wrong chord, go in and correct them, and then go right back to reading the paper," said Jack.

For Jimmy, listening to his father play the banjo would have a profound impact. He was clearly paying attention to every detail, even to the way his father would carefully remove the instrument from what he described as its "beguiling casement with alligator texture and silver clasps." Years later, as an established performer, he would tell his audiences he chose to become a guitar player because of the way his mother looked at his father when he played that "thing."

Following their father's interest, both Jimmy and Jack took to playing stringed instruments. Jimmy started with the ukulele, played the mandolin, and eventually became serious with the guitar. Jack took up the baritone ukulele. Their first public performance was at the holiday

Christmas party for Orlando Federal Savings and Loan. Their father was designing buildings for the bank. The boys performed mostly country songs and folk ballads as well as some of the songs taught to them by their father, including "Samson and Delilah" and "Kipling's Lady."

It was, by most accounts, a fairly typical childhood in the 1940s and early 1950s. There were girls, parties, music, and school.

Socially, Jimmy showed no signs of being an extrovert or someone who would one day command the attention of an adoring public. If anything, he was somewhat modest and reserved, as recalled by Syd Chase, a childhood acquaintance of both Jimmy and Bruce McEwan. "He was not a loud, boisterous individual," Chase said. "He was a very polite, civil person who always appeared to be relaxed and totally under control."

There was certainly no indication that the high school escapades of some of Jimmy's classmates at Winter Park High School would one day make their way into the annals of Florida folklore, such as the humorous yet macabre Maitland turkey farm massacre.

The story's protagonist, Hutto Proudfoot, is based on Jimmy's real-life best friend in high school, whose nickname was "The Bear." As the story goes, Hutto

> pulled up adjacent to the teeming turkey pens on the eve of Thanksgiving, leaned out of his rump sprung Henry J. automobile and blew three authoritative toots on a tin plated police whistle, causing the somnolent and semi comatose birds amassed there in holiday profusion to rouse themselves, poking their heads up periscope-wise to discover the source of the disturbance. Whereupon our young pilgrim leaned carefully out of his rusted chariot with an unplugged J.C. Higgins 10-gauge goose gun with which he slew 497 birds. This was referred to thereafter by the chroniclers of our community destiny as the Great Maitland Turkey Farm Massacre of Nineteen and Fifty-Three.

The Thanksgiving tale is included as a selection in the 1982 book *Every Night at Five: Susan Stamberg's All Things Considered Book.*

Other Winter Park landmarks, images, and people from Jimmy's childhood resurfaced more than twenty years later in vignettes of nostalgia to amuse and entertain audiences: Saturday matinees at the Baby Grand Theater at 122 South Park Street, decorated in "renaissance redneck"; Trudy Butram, the high school prom queen in the angora sweater who was a "teenage princess, sovereign subject of a hundred million fervent postpubescent ruminations and fantasies"; and of course Miss Eulalah Singleterry, the six and a half foot tall homeroom teacher "who loomed above us like a myopic praying mantis."

As a teenager in Winter Park, Jimmy was considered to be a good athlete. He loved to water ski on the lake and participated in high school sports. On one occasion, while attempting to break the school's record in the high jump, he went over the bar and missed the pit, landing on his tailbone. He had trouble walking for several days. After visits to a number of specialists, Jimmy was seen by his general practitioner, who diagnosed him with an adolescent arthritis that, without treatment, could eventually result in the fusing of his spine. The diagnosis was found to be independent of the high-jump injury. It was a condition that would plague him for the rest of his life.

In high school, it meant the end of all athletic activities and an afternoon ritual of coming home and lying down on the floor under a semicircular stainless steel reflector with light bulbs inside to generate heat. While his peers spent time at various after-school activities, Jimmy spent his afternoons prone on the floor reading anything he could get his hands on and practicing the guitar. "More signs of a misspent youth" is how he later described these years.

He read just about anything, from the classics to the massive *Webster's Dictionary* in his family's home. He was warned to keep his back straight for fear of having his spine fused. At the time, Jimmy was close to achieving his Eagle Scout Badge from the Boy Scouts. He lacked only the completion of the athletic merit badge. When the troop leader offered to make an exception due to his back condition, Jimmy would have nothing of it. If he couldn't complete it like everyone else, he wouldn't accept the badge.

It was part of a selfless character trait that was already starting to emerge.

"If there was a harder way to do something, Jimmy would usually find it," said Jack. "He was very independent and not particularly concerned with what other people thought."

The physical limitations of his back condition did not deter Jimmy's academic success or popularity at Winter Park High School. He was the senior class president, a member of the National Honor Society, and the associate editor of the school's yearbook. He might have been elected Student Council president if he hadn't voted for his opponent.

"Being the gentleman he was, he voted for the other guy," remembered Jack. "He figured the other guy was going to vote for him anyway and they would cancel each other out." Turns out his opponent voted for himself, resulting in a tie. Jimmy eventually lost by one vote in the runoff.

"It was characteristic of him putting other people first," said Jack. "Maybe it was a kind of chivalry or something else. He just wasn't going to put himself on center stage. It showed up all the way back then."

His southern charm and chivalry did not go unnoticed by Joan Abendroth (married name Pratt), the school's valedictorian and Jimmy's date to the senior prom. "He was a very proper gentleman," she said. "He was so creative and funny, and he loved sharing his talent with all of us."

There were frequent parties at Temple Grove. "The house was always open to lots of kids and to having a good time," Joan remembered. Inevitably the parties ended with Jimmy and Jack playing music and everyone singing along.

The trappings of his upper-middle-class upbringing seemed to matter little, Joan recalled. "He had zero patience with snobbery," she said. "He would be as kind to a gardener as to someone in high social standing in Winter Park. He just never thought someone's social standing was all that important. It was more about the person and trying to connect with them."

She continued, "He was a keen observer of people, and I can say in the years I knew him, he never deliberately hurt anyone. He was always wanting to help people in a kind and gentle manner."

The night of the high school prom, Joan hosted a pre-prom party at her house. All the guests arrived dressed for the prom, except for

Jimmy, who was a no-show. "He finally called and said the cleaners had lost his tuxedo pants and he was desperately trying to find a new pair of pants," she remembered. "I told him just find a pair of black pants because everyone else was here." Jimmy arrived shortly thereafter in a newfound pair of pants and holding a beautiful black orchid in hand. "I was just awed," she said.

By the end of high school, Jimmy was expanding on the musical influences of his father and becoming increasingly proficient with the guitar. He was particularly taken with the fingerpicking styles of guitar legends Merle Travis and Chet Atkins, and he began in earnest to study their techniques. Like other teenagers of the day he was mesmerized and energized by the charisma of a young Elvis Presley, whom he saw perform live at the Orlando Municipal Coliseum in 1953.

Meanwhile, Jimmy's daily afternoon back treatments were giving him ample time to read. He was developing an appreciation for the English language and building an expansive vocabulary that would in time become one of his signature traits.

And he was drawing on the influences and images of his youthful summers spent on the family's farm in the hills of the Nacoochee Valley of Georgia.

4

~~~~~~

If you want to study philosophy, you have to go to a primitive place.

GAMBLE ROGERS, "BEAN CREEK ALPHABET"

THE FAMILY FARM in northern Georgia where the Rogers clan gathered every summer wasn't exactly a primitive place. But it was fertile ground for experiencing and learning the lessons of a rural, agrarian lifestyle. It was a long way from the day-to-day life in Winter Park, Florida.

The Nacoochee Valley lies in the Appalachian foothills about ninety miles northeast of Atlanta. Originally populated by Native Americans, the valley is steeped in history and rich in culture. It was the scene of a gold rush in the early 1800s and soon inhabited by those who made a living growing and selling wheat, corn, apples, and cotton. There were also those who worked in the sawmills, jug factories, and distilleries.

Following the devastation inflicted by the Civil War, some areas of the valley recovered in large measure due to the opening of the Southern Railway in 1873. Yet seven decades later, the Nacoochee Valley still maintained its rural, rustic charm when Shelby Smith, the maternal grandfather of Jimmy and Jack Rogers, bought the family farm in White County, Georgia, soon after America's entry into World War II. Smith was an established businessman and entrepreneur named in *The Standard History of Georgia and Georgians* as "one of the substantial citizens and businessmen of Atlanta."

"He knew the men would be involved in the war effort, and he wanted a place where the women and grandchildren could gather in a secure and self-supporting way," Jack Rogers recalled.

It was a working farm, so the family had access to the various foods and goods that were being rationed during the war effort. Crops were harvested and canned in the nearby Sautee Valley cannery, while farm animals provided the basics like the bacon and butter.

The boys worked with the men in the morning and spent the afternoons roaming the vast expanse of the farm and the adjacent properties. Much like their life back home at Temple Grove, there was freedom to explore as they pleased. The sights and sounds of these youthful summers would one day come to life in the form of an anachronistic folklore portrayed on the stages of smoky taverns, college campuses, and folk festivals in the 1970s and 1980s.

"That's where a lot of the stories would come from," said Jack Rogers. For instance, Erindale's Feed Store in nearby Clarksville, Georgia, served as the mythical model for Erindale's Purina Store, where you could get a lot more than just chickens. You could get philosophy at Erindale's, where a circle of rusticated sages would gather around the loading ramp to espouse such popular aphorisms as "Life is what happens to you when you are making other plans."

From the time they were small children until they went away to college, the Rogers brothers' routine was the same. Jimmy, Jack, and their cousins would leave city life to spend the summers at the family farm with the women and a few hired hands like Moses, the caretaker, and Pauline, the cook. The men stayed back and tended to the family businesses. They would visit the farm briefly to stock up on food and then return home to carry on with their professions.

Lyn Rogers Lacey, Jimmy's daughter, said, "It was a kind of a dual existence that helped define my father. The farm was the inspiration for my daddy writing and singing about Habersham County Mephistopheles, Bean Creek, Shelby III, and the Brahma Bull. It was all there."

The farm inspired such youthful tales as Jimmy and his boy cousins ghosting from tree to tree to spy at night on the Sky Lake Campfire Girls, whom the folksinger later described as a "smorgasbord of prepubescent sensuality." The boy cousins were all "simultaneously smitten with the sap of blood lust" better known as puberty. "It was like the first time you held a boa constrictor," Gamble Rogers would one day tell his audiences. "You don't know if you are holding the snake or that mother's holding you. But you flat know something's gotcha."

Summers spent on the expansive family farm with first cousins no more than two years apart could only lead to childhood shenanigans. There were plenty of them, some of which were aimed directly at the family's beloved cook, Pauline.

"Daddy and Pauline had a very special relationship," said Lyn. "She had his number, and he knew how to test her limits."

Pauline was part Cherokee Indian and full of superstitions, some of which became the source and inspiration for the Gamble Rogers song "Blood Mountain." Blood Mountain lies a little southwest of Brasstown Bald and is the highest point of the Appalachian Trail in Georgia. Legend describes it as an Indian battleground where fighting was so intense the blood literally ran down its wooded slopes.

"The mystery and the spirit of the song springs from a conversation Jimmy had with Pauline when the six boy cousins discovered a water moccasin wedged in the nozzle of a fountain in front of the farmhouse," Jack recalled during a tribute to his brother at the 1992 Florida Folk Festival. "When Pauline arrived the serpent was one-third extended from the pipe literally grinning at the boys gathered around it." For Pauline it was an ominous sign. What ensued was a conversation with the cook about spirits and shadows that found its way into Gamble Rogers's "Blood Mountain" lyrics.

Far beyond Blood Mountain, I move by shadows bound.
Where the snake's head grins and the gray hawk tends the ground.

Pauline, the motherly cook, baked bread and pies every day for the family and placed them under a window in the kitchen. One day the cousins were particularly bored and thought the freshly baked bread loaf would be great for some target practice. They had to move in secrecy. "If you got in the crosshairs of Pauline, you couldn't sit down for days," said Lyn.

The boys removed the loaf, took it out to a tree stump, and commenced with their target practice. When they were done, they took great care to remove all the birdshot and covertly returned the loaf to its place under the window. Uncle Tom, who was the family patriarch on duty that summer, completed the meal blessings and prepared to partake of the day's bread. The boys looked on anxiously, hoping they had successfully removed all the birdshot. Uncle Tom bit down on the bread and instantly broke a tooth. He began blurting out a slew of words even Jimmy and his boy cousins had never heard before. "All the mothers grabbed their children away from the table, covering their ears," said Lyn, recounting the chaotic scene described by her father.

Pauline was meticulous about keeping the children from tracking in the Georgia clay, but that didn't stop Jimmy from arriving for a midday meal by riding the horse General Lee straight into the farmhouse hallway and announcing, "You told me not to bring my muddy feet into the house, so I decided to bring in the horse's muddy feet instead."

Life on the farm was not restricted to the three-story house and the five cabins. There was land to explore and life lessons to be learned, many of which would help define the persona of an observant boy who was to become a storytelling troubadour. It was the integrity and craftsmanship of the self-sufficient culture he encountered in the Nacoochee Valley that seemed to matter most.

"The people up there were well known for doing just about anything but getting everything right in the English language," said Jack. "Jimmy certainly never judged that. He loved that culture."

The farm has gone through several iterations and reconfigurations but remains in the Rogers family. It is still known simply as "the farm." At one point, Evelyn Rogers made a futile attempt to name it Hill Creek Farm, even going so far as to have stationery printed with that name. A small sign for Hill Creek Farm was erected near the property entrance, but that name never took.

As an adult, Gamble Rogers would often return to the family farm with his own children, always drawing references for his ever-evolving characters and stories. Once, he and his daughter Lyn took a walk to a covered bridge near the farm. As he gazed up at the carved initials and other graffiti he saw the inscription "Chester the Molester." He turned to Lyn and said, "Now that's good!" It wasn't long before Chester the Molester became a part of his show's storytelling repertoire.

5

Always dream and shoot higher than you know you can do. Do not bother just to be better than your contemporaries or predecessors. Try to be better than yourself.

—WILLIAM FAULKNER, *Paris Review*, 1956

BY THE TIME HE ENROLLED at the University of Virginia in the fall of 1955, James Gamble Rogers IV had developed a variety of interests. He was an avid reader with an appreciation for the classics and had expressed some interest in philosophy. Armed with an expansive vocabulary, he was beginning to show signs of becoming a talented writer in his own right. Of course, there was the ever-present family architecture legacy, which was the presumed career path. And there was the guitar.

His dedication and pursuit of perfection found its focal point with the acoustic guitar. Without much formal training he was already surpassing the boundaries of an occasional hobbyist. He was a student of the six-string and was learning both its history and technique. He was an early disciple of the syncopated finger-picking style of the great Merle Travis, the Kentucky-born country-western singer known for songs like "Sixteen Tons" and "Dark as a Dungeon" depicting the lives of coal miners. Jimmy practiced with a disciplined regimen, often two or three hours a day. As a result, he was becoming increasingly proficient.

The mid- to late 1950s was a time of revival for American folk music in coffeehouses and on college campuses across North America, especially on the East Coast. With groups like the Weavers, with Pete

Seeger, leading the way and the cauldron brewing in Greenwich Village, the folk revolution was on and about to explode.

While not exactly comfortable playing in public, Jimmy was making the rounds as a regular at UVA fraternity parties. It was a familiar, comfortable environment, and his hard work and talent as a guitar player were definitely being noticed. His brother, also a student at UVA, remembered a night the popular folk group the Kingston Trio performed on campus. After the concert one of the members of the trio came back to the fraternity house.

"He'd had a few drinks and someone put a guitar in his hand," Jack said of the visiting musician. "Somebody else asked Jimmy to get out his guitar and play with him. My brother politely declined because he would have absolutely shamed him. He wasn't going to put himself in a position of upstaging someone else."

During his first two years at UVA, Jimmy maintained his romantic relationship with his high school prom date, Joan Abendroth, who was attending Rollins College in Winter Park. On Easter weekend of their sophomore year, she visited Jimmy at UVA, where they were pinned. "I was serenaded as the sweetheart of Sigma Chi," Joan said with pride. She also remembered it as a time when Jimmy was working through the major conflict of what to do with his life.

"He was becoming more and more drawn into music, and coming from a family of architects and scholars, it was very hard for him to figure out what he was going to do," she said. "He didn't want to disappoint his parents at all. He was such a sensitive and caring man. Jimmy always knew music was where his heart was. It was just trying to figure out how to get there."

Joan was also keenly aware of the physical issues Jimmy was experiencing with his back. "It really hampered his movements," she said. "He was on a lot of aspirin and it would upset his stomach. He was probably fortunate that he never developed an ulcer, but he didn't dwell on it and he didn't want to talk about it. He just carried on. He didn't want any sympathy, but I could always tell when it was bothering him."

Jimmy and Joan were "unpinned" later that summer when it became apparent that Jimmy was becoming increasingly interested in pursuing a music career. The lifestyle of an entertainer was the issue.

"It just wouldn't have been a good fit for me," said Joan. "I lived a pretty traditional life. Jimmy and I had many wonderful times together but I was very much aware of the draw and pull that music had on him. I'm so glad he was able to figure it out and do what really made him happy." Their romantic relationship ended cordially, and the two stayed in touch until their paths diverged years later.

While he continued to make strides with his musical ambitions at UVA, academics remained somewhat a challenge. During his three and a half years at UVA, Jimmy changed majors three times, switching between architecture, English, and philosophy.

"I wouldn't say he had a checkered college career at Virginia, because he learned a lot," said Maggie Rogers, his first wife. "He just never liked taking exams."

Three decades after attending UVA, Gamble Rogers offered his own perspective in a 1987 interview with *Florida Magazine*. "There were a number of areas of study I could have pursued," Rogers said of his academic endeavors. "But they required time commitments I wasn't prepared to make and I was convinced I needed to move on with my life."

It was a lesson he may have learned directly from one of the most celebrated writers of the twentieth century, William Faulkner. The Nobel Prize laureate and Pulitzer winner Faulkner was already firmly established as a literary giant when he accepted a two-year appointment as a writer in residence at the University of Virginia in 1957. If ever a writer symbolized the South, it was Faulkner. His often tragic, apocryphal tales were spun with a stream of consciousness that explored and challenged the human spirit. He tackled race and slavery and wrote of outcasts and elitists. Many of his Southern Gothic tales were set in the fictitious Yoknapatawpha County, Mississippi, his native state.

During his tenure at the University of Virginia Faulkner gave lectures, many of which were recorded and have since been digitally preserved. He was often seen around campus, and he kept open office hours.

The circumstances of Rogers meeting Faulkner at UVA are somewhat shrouded in mystery. There are different versions of the story, no two of which are exactly the same, a recurring theme of the folksinger's own life story.

One of the more publicly circulated accounts was told to Jacksonville resident Jack Milne, who said he heard the story from Rogers himself in the 1980s, long after the singer-songwriter was well established and going by the name Gamble. Milne, a Civil War buff and school administrator, was a fan of Rogers and especially of his rendition of the song "The Kennesaw Line" written by Don Oja Dunaway.

Milne was in St. Augustine to meet with Gamble's friend Paul Berger, a well-known and highly respected luthier who was making a guitar for Milne's daughter Caroline.

"Paul Berger invited my daughter Caroline and me to have lunch with Gamble at the Gypsy Cab Company," said Milne. "I remember Gamble taking the time to show my daughter the right way to spin spaghetti on the fork. It was very touching."

After lunch, Rogers invited Milne and his daughter to come by his house, a short distance from the restaurant. "He showed me his boat and some old rifles he had from his dad," Milne said. "It was all very casual. We stayed at the house for a couple of hours."

They took some pictures and talked about guitars, guns, and Faulkner. Here is how Milne remembered Rogers telling the story:

Every day Faulkner held regular office hours between one and two. I went up there several times, and there would always be a line to sit with the master. I would never wait around because I thought it was silly to do so and secondly, I didn't want to wait in line. But one day I was up there for something else and his door was open and he was sitting at his desk reading a book. So I knocked on the door and asked, "Professor Faulkner, are you seeing students today?" He told me just to take a seat and he'd be with me shortly. So, I sat down across the desk, and he's just sitting there reading a book and about fifteen or twenty minutes go by. I didn't know if he'd forgotten about me or was testing me. Should I say something? Should I offer to come back another time, or should I keep my mouth shut? About five minutes later, Faulkner closes his book, opens his desk drawer, and goes, "Man I wrote some good shit back then. Now, what can I do for you?"

There were no specific details of what happened next.

What did happen next, said Rogers's daughter Lyn, was a turning point, although she openly acknowledged she never heard the story directly from her father. The account she was told was that while at UVA, Rogers made several passes by Faulkner's private office door but could never muster the courage to knock: "He would basically chicken out at the last minute until one day Faulkner opened his door and asked, 'Son, are you coming in today or not?'" After they talked for a moment Rogers explained he was studying architecture because that was expected of him but his real desire was to become a musician and a writer, at which point Faulkner chastised him for not being true to himself.

"He had intuitively come to the place of his own moment of truth," said Lyn. "He knew he was at a crossroads, and I think the love of music and writing just eventually overtook him."

Maggie Rogers told yet another version of the meeting. She said that while at Virginia, Faulkner and Rogers met regularly outside the area liquor store, where they would sit and hold court with the locals who were cashing their checks and buying booze.

"Faulkner influenced a lot of what he did," said Maggie, "especially his love for writing."

Whatever the circumstances of their interactions, the Faulkner influence was palpable. Like Faulkner, Rogers created a mythical county in his native state as a setting for his Southern Gothic tales. He even paid tribute to the master with his story "Airstream Trailer Orgy," chronicled from the minutes of the Third Annual Snipes Ford William Faulkner Literary Society convocation, a trailer park event attended by Agamemnon Jones, Still Bill, Chester the Molester, and Forklift Mary, among others. "Lovers of literature, each and every one," Rogers described them.

Rogers's restlessness with formal education eventually got the best of him. He left the University of Virginia without a degree, or as his family would say, "He was excused from the university." Music lessons with legendary blues guitarist Charlie Byrd in nearby Washington, DC, took priority over final exams.

In typical fashion, Rogers summarized his college experience with his own astute observation that he "never learned how to do anything more than to make the Doppler effect on a flat-top guitar."

6

~~~~~~~~~~~~~~~~

Read, read, read. Read everything—trash, classics, good and bad, and see how they do it. Just like a carpenter who works as an apprentice and studies the master. Read! You'll absorb it.

Then write. If it's good, you'll find out. If it's not, throw it out of the window.

—WILLIAM FAULKNER, UNIVERSITY OF MISSISSIPPI, 1947

ALTHOUGH HE RETURNED to Winter Park in 1958 without a degree, James Gamble Rogers IV was not entirely through with formal education. He enrolled in a writing course at Rollins College and began work on a novel. It was a period of creative exploration for the twenty-one-year-old Rogers, who also continued to practice and perfect his guitar-playing skills.

His talent as a writer and a thinker did not go unnoticed. His creative writing professor at Rollins College was the noted American author Edwin Granberry.

Granberry was a close friend and confidant of Margaret Mitchell, author of *Gone with the Wind*. On the day of its publication in 1936, Granberry wrote a glowing review of the book for the *New York Sun*, comparing it to Tolstoy's *War and Peace*. It was the beginning of a close, personal friendship between Granberry and Mitchell.

As a professor at Rollins, Granberry believed he had seen an extraordinary talent in his creative writing student Jimmy Rogers. He said as much in a letter of recommendation he wrote to Stetson University on behalf of Rogers, who would make one last attempt to finish school and obtain a degree.

"I know James so well and I think so highly of his most unusual intellectual potential that I cannot refrain from doing all I can to assist him in his determination to complete his college work," Granberry wrote on July 31, 1959.

As for his association with Rogers, Granberry wrote, "I made the discovery that I had in my keeping the most pronounced writing talent of my twenty-five years of teaching. Furthermore, I made the discovery that the profundity of this boy's thinking was so far beyond what we normally encounter in the college student, that I saw quickly what had caused some of Jim's restlessness and impatience with certain phases inevitable with college life."

Granberry concluded his letter with the hope that his interactions with the young student had given Rogers an "appreciation of the very fine talent he has been endowed with; a better understanding of how to put it to use for the betterment of mankind as well as of himself."

Rogers was accepted at Stetson. Once again, however, he left without completing the course work. Nor did he, to anyone's knowledge, ever complete the novel he had been writing.

"I wouldn't be surprised if he destroyed the manuscript," said his brother, Jack. "He just said he wasn't ready. I'm sure he was judging his work against Faulkner."

Rogers's passion for music, however, was unfaltering, and he was beginning to surround himself with those of a like mind.

Paul Champion may have been Jimmy's first and closest musical contemporary. Born in 1938 in the Panama Canal Zone to a military family, Champion was an accomplished banjo player by his early teens. A protege of bluegrass legends Earl Scruggs and Don Remo, Champion won a national amateur banjo contest around the same time he was accepted to West Point Military Academy. A heart murmur discovered during his admission physical resulted in his being rejected for military service.

Champion went on to attend Florida State University in Tallahassee. Jimmy had also been spending time in Tallahassee, where he had met Maggie Whitehead, who was soon to become his first wife.

In Champion, Rogers found a kindred spirit and his musical equivalent. Although they came from different backgrounds, they found a common bond with music. Champion at an early age was certainly the more experienced, having already played publicly with the Log Cabin Boys bluegrass band as a teenager. The two spent considerable time together playing music and began making serious plans to open their own coffeehouse.

They would find some inspiration at the savory cafe Le Collage in St. Augustine. A self-proclaimed bohemian, Dan Holiday opened the cafe in the fall of 1959 with the help of a friend, Augie Demello, who had been living in Greenwich Village and was familiar with the emerging coffeehouse scene. Augie had slick-talked his way into acquiring a 1923 La Pavonie expresso machine with a winged lion on the top that had been the property of Cafe Figaro, a Beat Generation hangout on the corner of MacDougal and Bleecker Street in the Village.

"The week before we opened, Augie drove down from New York and delivered this expresso machine," Holiday wrote in a self-published biography in 2003. "What a treasure. Augie also set me up with a weekly shipment from Greenwich Village of a special blend of expresso coffee and some copies of the *Village Voice* newspaper, which was pretty radical for St. Augustine at that time."

The menu at Le Collage featured a thirty-cent expresso described as a "drink which brings back the cobbled piazza of Capri." The expresso machine has remained a piece of St. Augustine lore and sits on display at Theo's Restaurant on the San Sebastian River just off of US Highway 1.

Le Collage became a popular spot for performers on the underground circuit between Greenwich Village and St. Augustine, Holiday said.

One day, these kids arrived on our doorstep with a guitar and banjo in hand. It was Jim Rogers and Paul Champion. It was the first time they had ever played in St. Augustine. Paul was so bashful he played banjo with his back to the audience . . . all six of us! Paul played "Foggy Mountain Breakdown," and Jimmy played the guitar but had not started his Gamble Rogers singing stories at the time. They had come from Tallahassee to pick our brains about the coffeehouse business. They wanted to open their own cafe.

Holiday and some friends eventually drove to Tallahassee to help Rogers and Champion open a cafe, which they named the Baffled Knight.

One of the waitresses working at Le Collage at the time was a young Doris Mowrey, who would be the subject of one of Rogers's most poignant and poetic songs following her mysterious death in downtown St. Augustine in 1963. The song "Doris" was always introduced with a heart-rending portrayal of the slain protagonist.

Holiday was one of St. Augustine's more colorful characters in the 1960s. According to his autobiography, *Just Plane Dumb Luck*, he resided for a time in the city's historic lighthouse through a rental agreement with the US Coast Guard. He worked for the NBC TV network as a bodyguard during civil rights unrest and sat on the St. Johns County grand jury that investigated Martin Luther King Jr.'s activities in St. Augustine. Holiday became well known as a sandal maker and leather craftsman, eventually opening a leather shop on Aviles Street in St. Augustine.

Although both were relatively shy, Rogers and Champion were musical complements, blending their sounds with a unique chemistry that was continuing to build. They cavorted together around St. Augustine, Tallahassee, Winter Park, and Orlando. Many of their escapades over the next twenty years became legendary in Florida folk circles.

Champion rarely spoke on stage and preferred to let his banjo do the talking, but he had his own penchant for mischief. Once while dining at a restaurant in St. Augustine, Champion kept his eye on a fish that seemed a little too large for the establishment's aquarium. After dining, he paid his bill, reached into the tank, grabbed the fish and headed straight for the nearby Bridge of Lions, where he tossed the slippery catch into the more expansive waters, all the while being chased by a group of vigilantes who thought he left without paying for his meal.

7

YOUNG JIMMY ROGERS and his family were frequent visitors to the state capital in Tallahassee. His father's burgeoning architecture practice had grown well beyond the boundaries of Winter Park. The design expertise of James Gamble Rogers II was in big demand for churches, courthouses, colleges, and government buildings. A prominent accomplishment was his classical design of the state Supreme Court building, which was dedicated in 1948. The building, encompassing 55,000 square feet, has a plaque in the lobby honoring his work as its architect.

It was in Tallahassee that Jimmy Rogers met Maggie Whitehead, who eventually became his first wife.

"Actually, we were friends who got married" is the way Maggie remembered it.

Maggie was raised in Tallahassee with her three sisters and two aunts living in the family home. Maggie had extended family in the Florida Panhandle, some with political connections. Her father's first cousin was F. Wilson Carraway, a state senator from Leon County.

Although Maggie said she remembered meeting Jimmy as a child, they didn't start seeing each other regularly until after he left the University of Virginia and returned to Florida.

"I always called him Gamble," she said. "That's what he wanted to be called."

Early on, Maggie was a strong advocate and supporter of his musical pursuits. She recalled, "His father was a very good musician, but he played socially and never intended to do it professionally, and I don't think either of Gamble's parents intended for him to do it professionally. The truth of the matter is that sometimes it got a little difficult, and probably I stood between them a lot."

Far from a struggle, Maggie characterized his move toward music more as Gamble "just trying to put one foot ahead of the other, just like the rest of us."

His first serious attempt at establishing a career as a musician came when he and Champion opened the Baffled Knight coffeehouse in the early 1960s. The small basement cafe was under a firehouse on North Adams Street in downtown Tallahassee, not too distant from the Florida State University campus.

Maggie said the cafe was named after the traditional English poem "The Baffled Knight," which had long been set to music and become a popular folk ballad. "That was a song that Gamble got from his dad," she said.

> There was a knight was drunk with wine,
> A riding along the way, sir;
> And there he met with a lady fine,
> Among the cocks of hay, sir.
>
> "Shall you and I, O lady faire,
> Among the grass lye down-a,
> And I will have a special care
> Of rumpling of your gown-a?"

The house band at the Baffled Knight consisted of Rogers, Champion, and a third musician named Charles "Chuck" Glore. Glore had earned a music scholarship at Stetson University, where he was also editor of the school paper. With a gifted voice and talent as a skilled guitar and piano player, Glore worked his way through college performing as a soloist before joining Rogers and Champion at the Baffled Knight.

The trio was sometimes referred to as the Baffled Knights, but they officially called themselves the Salty Dogs, after the early 1900s folk song "Salty Dog Blues":

> I want to be your salty dog
> Or I won't be your man at all,
> Honey let me be your salty dog

"It was sort of their theme song," said Maggie.

The group, often sporting blazers and skinny neckties, performed nightly, mostly with a mixture of popular folk songs and bluegrass tunes. The set list would invariably include a couple of original songs performed by Rogers. One such was "The Black Label Blues," in which he crooned about the whiskey Jack Daniels being the cure-all for the fears, pains, and sorrows of life.

Despite operating in a dry county, the Baffled Knight became a popular spot in Tallahassee. The band of talented musicians developed a loyal following who spread the word around town about the Salty Dogs. Among those who dropped in to check out the young trio was Florida folk-singing legend Will McLean, widely acknowledged as the father of Florida folk music. The friendship they developed over the years would have a great influence on Rogers's life.

By now, Rogers was starting to use the first name Gamble interchangeably with Jimmy. While his family and childhood friends still called him Jimmy, he was becoming better known as Gamble in his music circles. If he were to ever succeed as a musician, the name Jimmie Rodgers was already associated with the great singer-songwriter from the early 1930s known as the father of country music. There was also Jimmie F. Rodgers, a contemporary who established himself in the late 1950s as a pop entertainer with his hit recording "Honeycomb," which had climbed to the top of the *Billboard* charts.

"The name Gamble Rogers had such a ring to it that it just seemed to fit perfectly," said Tony Perry, a friend of Maggie's who met Rogers at the Baffled Knight. Tony Perry and his brother John were in Tallahassee in the early 1960s working on a band of their own called the Moonshiners. Tony Perry said,

> A fellow in the music department at FSU, kind of a folkie guy, mentioned Gamble specifically and said you have to go down to the Baffled Knight and hear this guy. Well, it knocked me out. They were fabulous. Chuck Glore and Gamble sang a lot of two-part harmonies while Paul Champion chimed in with a banjo breakdown at super speed. Gamble used to say that Paul Champion played the banjo "full." The goal was to play it as fast as you could, but clearly.

John Perry added, "Paul had such a unique character that went into his banjo playing. No one played the banjo like Paul Champion."

Tony and John Perry said they were aware of Gamble's family background. After all, the small stage of the Baffled Knight coffeehouse was only blocks away from the steps of the majestic Florida Supreme Court building that Gamble's father designed.

The Perry brothers had their own family pressures as aspiring musicians. John remembered being asked, "Are you really going to go on the road and do this kind of thing?" It was a familiar question for a new generation looking for their own identity in a changing culture. It was about the same time that Bob Dylan was admonishing parents, "Your sons and your daughters are beyond your command" in his song "The Times They Are a-Changin'."

"I just think Gamble knew he was going to play music," said John Perry. "It was a gift that should not be ceased."

While the Salty Dogs never recorded an album, they did appear as background musicians in a 1964 blood-splatter film entitled *2,000 Maniacs*, directed by Herschell Gordon Lewis, often referred to as "the godfather of gore." Lewis, from Chicago, was known for directing a series of 1960s low-budget, blood-curdling films with titles like *Blood Feast*, *The Wizard of Gore*, and *The Gore-Gore Girls*. His movie *2,000 Maniacs* was filmed on location in St. Cloud, Florida.

"Herschell Lewis made a bet with a friend he could do this low-budget movie and make a million dollars," said Maggie Rogers. "The deal was they were never going to do any remakes because they couldn't afford to."

The plot loosely revolves around some Yankee tourists being lured to the fictional southern town of Pleasant Valley for a centennial celebration, when things go horribly wrong. The vengeful spirits inhabiting the town exact blood-thirsty revenge on their unsuspecting northern guests.

"Madmen Crazed for Carnage. An Entire Town Bathed in Pulsating Human Blood," screams the movie trailer. All the while, the distinctive banjo and guitar-picking sounds of the Salty Dogs can be heard clearly in the background. The movie starred *Playboy* magazine's Connie Mason, the June 1963 Playmate of the Month.

Gamble Rogers, Paul Champion, and Chuck Glore sing and play background music throughout the film and appear as strolling musicians in several scenes. While he is not listed in the performing credits, the cult film does provide some of the clearest and earliest images of Gamble Rogers the performer.

Years after it was released, Maggie Rogers remembered taking the family to see the film at the Winter Park drive-in: "We had a station wagon and took the kids, but nobody could see for some reason. So we put a blanket on top of the station wagon and watched the movie from up there."

In spite of the owners' best efforts, the Baffled Knight coffeehouse was never a financial success. "I think they just ran out of steam more than anything else," said Maggie. For Gamble and Maggie, it meant a move to Winter Park, where he would make one last attempt at architecture by day and folk singing by night.

8

Serendipity always rewards the prepared.

—KATORI HALL, "ROAD BACK TO RUSSIA"

ONE WOULD HAVE BEEN hard-pressed to have lived in Winter Park, Florida, in the early 1960s without having been keenly aware of the Rogers family and their significant impact on the community. The very ambiance and character of the town was suffused with the architectural designs and influences of James Gamble Rogers II. From the Spanish and French provincial residences to Rollins College and the many churches, retail shops, and apartment buildings, the design work of the Rogers family firm helped define the Winter Park community and the surrounding areas of Central Florida.

It was also clear that if he wanted, the opportunity to carry on the family's architecture legacy was available to the would-be folksinger after his return to Winter Park from the Baffled Knight in Tallahassee. "There's no doubt my brother would have been a very good architect," said Jack Rogers, who himself joined the family firm shortly after graduating from the University of Virginia.

For the next few years after leaving the Baffled Knight, Jimmy, who was now going by Gamble in his music circles, would try his hand at both architecture and folksinging. For a time Gamble worked at the family business, even though he had not obtained a college degree and was not a licensed architect. One of his memorable projects was a juvenile detention center in Orlando designed without bars. "It was a very forward-looking, humanistic design," said Jack. He also designed a chapel for the Sertoma Club that was based on Stonehenge. The chapel was never built because of a lack of funding.

At night and on weekends Gamble was moonlighting in various clubs and folk festivals in the area. One was the small cafe in Winter Park, the Carrera Room, that Maggie opened and operated as she continued to be supportive of her husband's musical pursuits. The two had been married at Temple Grove and were now raising three children, Chuck and Lolly and Lyn, the youngest, who was born to Gamble and Maggie in 1963.

They lived in a house on Knowles Avenue, literally next door to the family's architecture office in downtown Winter Park. While neither Chuck nor Lolly was Gamble's biological child, they most definitely considered him to be their dad. He shared with them a love for music and the wild outdoors. Lolly and Chuck were often given the freedom to roam and explore, much like Gamble and his brother a generation earlier.

"When I was a young child, I remember so many great things about my dad that really grew inside of me about loving the natural world," Lolly said. There were canoe trips in the nearby canal, making cane poles for fishing, and roaming around the orange groves at Temple Grove. "It had a huge impact on who I am now."

The residence on Knowles Avenue was also a house filled with music. Lolly fondly remembers the silly songs her dad played for her, like "Egyptian Ella," a traditional folk song about a dancing girl who started getting fat: "Every day saw three more pounds on Ella . . . and to make it worse she lost her fella."

Gamble and his musician friends like Paul Champion and folksinger Jim Ballew often gathered on the family porch and played music late into the night. Chuck recalled, "We all really loved Paul Champion. He was this big teddy bear of a guy who played an amazing banjo and guitar."

It was Champion who gave Chuck his first "official" guitar lesson by handing the seven-year-old a Martin D-45 guitar on the house porch and showing him how to play a basic chord. "That started to light the spark in me," said Chuck, a spark that would later ignite to full-blown fire when his dad taught him the chords to "House of the Rising Sun." Chuck, an accomplished musician, teaches music in St. Augustine.

As a young father, Gamble was already demonstrating a calm but commanding demeanor. "I was sort of a busy kid," said Chuck, adding that there were several occasions when his dad had to be called to pull him off a rooftop in downtown Winter Park.

"Chuuuck, now just come on down." That was really all he had to say. "I had too much respect for him to not listen," said Chuck.

In addition to moonlighting at area clubs in and around Winter Park, Gamble and Maggie frequently traveled to play in coffeehouses and cafes from New York to California, usually leaving the kids behind with family during their extended trips. Sometimes Maggie joined her husband on stage to sing harmonies. "In those early days, Gamble didn't like to perform on stage alone," Maggie said. "I don't know why, because he was so good." He was continuing to hone his skills as a songwriter and guitar player and was building his own loyal following in Central Florida.

At The Carrera Room in Winter Park, Gamble played to a packed room while Maggie served sandwiches and flavored coffee to the patrons. "It was a stopping-off point for musicians on their way to Miami," said Maggie. "Freddie Neil, Josh White, and others would stop in and then stay with us before heading south."

When Gamble and Maggie traveled to New York City, they stayed in Greenwich Village at the same apartment as the up-and-coming folksinger Phil Ochs. The singing journalist Ochs arrived in Greenwich Village in 1962 at the peak of the folk music revival. His apartment at 178 Bleecker Street became a meeting place and hangout for Village folk musicians.

"The door was always open, the traffic constant," Marc Eliot wrote in his biography of Ochs, *Death of a Rebel*. The regulars included Al Kooper, John Sebastian, Eric Andersen, Dave van Ronk, and Ochs's rival Bob Dylan.

"Bob Dylan was there all the time," said Maggie. "He and Gamble had a lot in common in that they were both good writers."

Their approach to writing songs, however, could not have been more different. "Gamble was very studied with everything he wrote," said Maggie. "He kept a thesaurus with him. That is not true of Dylan. Dylan just spit things out. It just flowed out of him."

Gamble would labor over a word and go back and forth, often using Maggie or someone nearby as a sounding board. He sometimes took months to write a song. "It was a struggle because he was such a perfectionist," said Maggie. She cites Gamble's song "Masterbuilders" as one whose ending changed so many times it "would make your head spin." His commitment to perfection and professionalism carried over to his practice habits. He continued to maintain a regimented routine of practicing at least two or three hours a day. "He even practiced scales," said Maggie.

Borrowing a phrase attributed to the Polish pianist and diplomat Ignacy Jan Paderewski, Gamble proclaimed, "If I miss a day of practicing, I notice it. If I miss two days, the critics notice. If I miss three days the audience notices."

While in the Village, Gamble played the usual circuit of folk clubs and coffeehouses. It was a magical time in Greenwich Village, which was attracting a generation of well-educated idealists and activists who were shedding their middle-class backgrounds and reinventing themselves on the streets and cafes within the confines of a few square blocks in New York City.

Back home in Winter Park, the attempt to work at the family's architecture firm by day and folksinging at night and on weekends was proving to be a hefty challenge. Maggie said such moonlighting was discouraged. By 1966 Gamble made a decision to leave the family business in pursuit of an architecture job with a new, innovative firm in Boston called the Cambridge Seven. There was an active music scene in Boston, and Gamble, who had performed in that city before, was hoping a change of scenery would be more conducive to his varying interests.

On the trip up to Boston, Gamble stopped in New York City, where he contacted his and Maggie's friend Tony Perry from Tallahassee during his days at the Baffled Knight. Tony's brother John had joined the popular folk group the Serendipity Singers. The nine-member ensemble scored a major hit with its debut single, "Don't Let Rain Come Down (Crooked Little Man)." The group was going through some personnel changes and having an audition to replace two guitar players. Tony, who was a vocalist, wanted to join his brother in the group but didn't play an instrument. He asked if Gamble would go with him to the audition and play the guitar.

The audition was held at the Bitter End in Greenwich Village. The nightclub was owned by Fred Weintraub, who managed the Serendipity Singers along with several other major folk artists. The Bitter End was a showcase for top folk acts like Peter, Paul, and Mary, Neil Diamond, Bob Dylan, Phil Ochs, and others.

"I had a pretty strong set prepared for the audition, but I didn't play an instrument," said Tony Perry. "Vocally, I had a huge falsetto top, so I could cover a lot of high notes, which is something the band needed. Gamble and I sort of came in to the audition as a pair."

Not surprisingly, Gamble blew them away with his guitar playing, so much so that the group decided they could do with one less guitar player, essentially making it possible for Tony Perry to join his brother in the group.

"We didn't have a lead guitar player," said John Perry. "And having six guys playing rhythm never made that much sense. It became apparent to [ensemble leader] Brian Sennent that with Tony and Gamble combined we would replace the guys that left and we would be very well off."

Gamble and Tony were hired by the Serendipity Singers on the spot.

"Gamble never even went back to Florida," said Tony. "We had a big apartment on West Tenth Street in the Village with a room in it that he could move right into and also use as a closet."

As a result of the impromptu audition, Gamble didn't complete his trip to Boston and the Cambridge Seven architecture firm.

"That was the end of the Boston adventure before it ever began," Maggie said. "He called me and he called them and that was it."

He also called his brother. "He wanted to tell me he was leaving architecture to play music," Jack said. "I was only a little surprised because he seemed enthusiastic about the architecture firm in Boston. But I always knew the music was there. If he had really wanted to practice architecture, he would have had to go back to school, and I was pretty sure that wasn't going to happen."

Interestingly, the Perry brothers said Gamble never mentioned anything to them about being on his way to an architecture job in Boston. "Oh my God, that's the first we've ever heard about that," said Tony Perry.

As for the family's reaction to Gamble's decision, Jack said, "Well, it's a hard way to earn a living. Most don't. I think it was a reasonable concern. But my father and my mother were both understanding."

Whatever external pressures there may have been, it was clear Gamble knew the pressure of expectations. He also knew it was the music that was in his heart. After years of conflict and struggle he had found the ticket to follow his dream.

The die had now been cast. Literally overnight, Gamble Rogers had been thrust into the world of professional entertainment with an established and successful folk group that was touring the county and preparing for its next appearance on *The Ed Sullivan Show*.

9

IN THE 1960S A MEASURE OF an entertainer's success could be judged by the number of appearances on *The Ed Sullivan Show*, television's longest-running variety show. The Serendipity Singers made their first appearance on *Ed Sullivan* on December 27, 1964, and were preparing for another when Gamble Rogers joined the group in 1966.

The singing ensemble got its start in a University of Colorado fraternity. Originally known as the Newport Singers, the group moved from Colorado to New York in the spring of 1963 hoping to land a recording contract. Under the management of the folk impresario Fred Weintraub, the group changed its name to the Serendipity Singers and soon became a regular headliner on *Hootenanny*, a weekly TV show filmed at various college campuses. They also signed a recording contract with Phillips Records.

Their hit song "Don't Let the Rain Come Down (Crooked Little Man)" reached number 6 on the *Billboard* magazine charts. They followed up with "Beans in My Ears," which was the source of some controversy since many interpreted the song's underlying message to be that teenagers need not listen to their parents.

The group was discouraged from playing the song when it made its 1964 debut on the Sullivan show. They opted instead for "Every Time I Feel Your Spirit," the title track from a popular Nat King Cole album. The other musical acts on the Sullivan show that evening were Diana Ross and the Supremes and Leslie Uggams.

With their clean-cut, preppy image, the Serendipity Singers drew unavoidable comparisons with the more popular New Christy Minstrels. But the group carved out its own niche and reached the peak of its popularity with the release of six albums in 1965–1966.

By the time Gamble Rogers and Tony Perry joined the group, folk music was on the verge of losing some of its commercial appeal. The country had been swept up by the British invasion, and Dylan had rocked the folk world by going electric at the 1965 Newport Folk Festival. The Serendipity Singers, however, remained very popular on college campuses and had a demanding concert schedule.

Maggie Rogers stayed behind with the children in Florida. She recalled,

> It was a tough time. They played so many concerts, maybe close to 300 a year. He just wasn't around. I used to take the children to see him if they were going to be in any one area for more than a few days. I piled the kids in the car once and drove all the way to St. Louis because they were going to be there for a week. The group was very successful, but I can tell you he never liked it all that much. He couldn't stand it when their guitars weren't in tune. He would walk over to one of them and tune it right in the middle of a song if he had to.

Gamble was making a living, though. The band members were paid an annual salary of $17,500, part of which went to expenses, John Perry said. The Perry brothers had vivid memories of their days on the road with Gamble.

"Gamble was not good with deadlines," said Tony. "He ran about thirty minutes behind the rest of the world."

"We used to give him a call about an hour before everyone else," said John. One time in particular, John kept pounding on Gamble's door as they were preparing to leave for the airport for the next concert destination. He came to the door in his underwear and said, "John, old buddy, you're just gonna have to go on without me."

He didn't care much for flying anyway, preferring to drive instead when at all possible. He was, however, one of the more dependable ones in the group. On at least two occasions half of the band members didn't show up, leaving Gamble and the two Perry brothers to carry the day.

"He was so intelligent and inner-directed," said John Perry. "I think he had a sense of otherness about him, that he was essentially different from everybody else he knew. And he was right. It wasn't something he bragged about at all."

Nor was he overly concerned with what others were doing around him, in the Village or anywhere else.

"Gamble was Gamble all the time," said Tony Perry. "He didn't get caught up in anything, including the whole flavor of how people were writing songs in that era, which was about politics and telling people what to do. Gamble was a folklorist through and through, and he stayed true to that. By the way, for as long as we knew him, he never debauched, although I'm sure he had an occasional drink or two."

For their appearance on *The Ed Sullivan Show* on January 7, 1967, the Serendipity Singers had prepared a three-song folk medley of "If I Were a Carpenter," "Elusive Butterfly," and "Who Am I." The show's lineup that evening included Ethel Merman, Gordon McRae, and comedians Flip Wilson and Myron Cohen.

"The Sullivan show was such a big deal you couldn't help but be anxious. The panic of it all was that it was dead live," said Tony Perry.

Myron Cohen, the Borscht Belt comedian and storyteller, had just finished his segment of the show when he walked past the anxious Serendipity Singers waiting in the wings. "Aw rrrright, vich von of you is Sarah?" Cohen asked. That broke the ice. The group hurried through their medley, after which Sullivan beckoned the two women in the group to join him center stage for another round of applause. "It all happened so fast I told Gamble I thought we left something out," said Tony Perry.

The Sullivan appearance was followed by another triumphant coast-to-coast tour of high school auditoriums and college campuses. The show had evolved to include some comedy sketches in addition to the group's full arrangement of pop-folk ballads and songs.

For Gamble, however, it was the beginning of the end with the Serendipity Singers. John Perry left the group shortly after the Sullivan appearance to pursue a career in acting. He appeared as the clean-shaven yet rugged sailor in Old Spice TV commercials in the 1970s. He is the father of the well known actor Matthew Perry of *Friends* fame. The two have appeared together as father and son in film and television.

At age thirty, Rogers was ready to move on from the role of a "hired gun," a term he used to describe his brief run with the Serendipity Singers. "Gamble used that term out of modesty," Tony Perry said. "Since we were not in the original group, he didn't want to take credit for the hit records, which was really the reason we were allowed to have the success we had. It was pretty evident that his talent was such that he could get plenty of bookings on his own."

For all of their success, the Serendipity Singers had become a show group of interchangeable faces lost in a 1960s folk music time warp. Gamble knew he had much more to offer. His departure from the Serendipity Singers after only a couple of years came with little fanfare.

Tony Perry remained a few years after his brother and Gamble left the group. The Perry brothers eventually reunited to play music as a duo in the Oja, California, area.

"His influence has never left us," said Tony Perry. "We still sing Gamble Rogers songs and tell Gamble Rogers stories. Because we traveled together with the Serendips, we got to know him well back then, but most people didn't even know who he was."

That was about to change. Gamble Rogers the folklorist was headed out on his own. He was about to harness the experiences of his youth and his keen observations of the human condition to give birth to Oklawaha County, a community of renaissance rednecks and rural alchemists, on his way to becoming Florida's cherished troubadour.

Gamble Rogers, late 1970s. Photo by Evon Streetman. *Florida Memory*, State Library and Archives of Florida. https://www.floridamemory.com/items/show/296652.

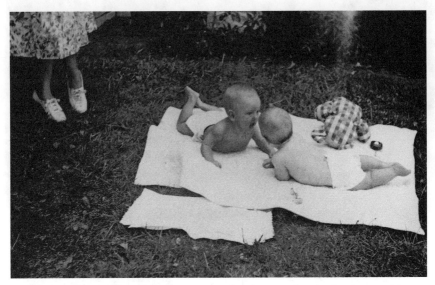

Gamble Rogers (*left*) and Bruce McEwan. The photo is dated July 16, 1937. Photo courtesy of Bruce and M. L. McEwan.

Gamble and newborn daughter, Lyn. Photo courtesy of Maggie Rogers.

Two little boys, Gamble (*standing*) and brother, Jack Rogers, playing by Lake Maitland in Winter Park. Photo provided by *Winter Park Magazine*. Courtesy of the Rogers family.

Gamble singing lead at the Tupperware Jubilee near Orlando, January 1964. Also pictured are Maggie Rogers (*second from left*) and Paul Champion (*far right*). Photo from the collection at PaulChampion.net, Bob Higginbotham, webmaster, used with permission.

Florida music festival. Pictured are (*from left*) Don Smith, Gamble Rogers, Liz Corrigan, Bob Patterson, and Paul Champion. Photo from the collection at Paul Champion.net, Bob Higginbotham, webmaster, used with permission.

Gamble with Maggie and family. In the photo are (*from left*) Gamble, Chuck, Lyn, Maggie, and Lolly. Courtesy of Maggie Rogers.

On stage at the Tradewinds Tropical Lounge, Gamble Rogers and Bob Patterson. Photo.courtesy of Bob Patterson.

Gamble Rogers and Bob Patterson outside the Tradewinds Tropical Lounge. Photo courtesy of Bob Patterson.

Gamble at the Hatchett Creek Music Festival, 1976. Photo courtesy of Kenneth M. Barrett Jr.

Gamble talking with his guitar hero Merle Travis at the Philadelphia Folk Festival. Courtesy of Bob Patterson.

Chicago singer-songwriter Steve Goodman and Gamble Rogers at the Philadelphia Folk Festival. Photo by Bob Penney, courtesy of Bob Patterson collection.

Gamble picking guitar in the living room of his Magnolia Drive home on Salt Run. Photo courtesy of the Rogers family.

Gamble telling a story, late 1970s. Photo by Robert S. Blount. *Florida Memory*, State Library and Archives of Florida. https://www.floridamemory.com/items/ show/296653.

Storyteller "Cousin" Thelma Boltin and Gamble Rogers at the 1982 Florida Folk Festival. Photo by John Marshall. *Florida Memory*, State Library and Archives of Florida, Florida Memory. https://www.floridamemory.com/items/show/320897.

Will McLean and Gamble Rogers at the 1982 Florida Folk Festival. *Florida Memory*, State Library and Archives of Florida. https://www.floridamemory.com/items/show/115487.

Gamble and granddaughter Neely waiting side stage at the 1985 Florida Folk Festival. *Florida Memory*, State Library and Archives of Florida. https://www. floridamemory.com/items/show/110402.

Paul Champion and Gamble Rogers at the 1985 Florida Folk Festival in White Springs. *Florida Memory*, State Library and Archives of Florida. https://www.floridamemory. com/items/show/110411.

Above: Gamble and Nancy. Photo courtesy of the Rogers family.

Left: Gamble and Nancy exchanging vows at their backyard wedding. Photo courtesy of the Rogers family.

Luthier Paul Berger displays the makings of a Gamble Rogers custom guitar.
Photo courtesy of the late Paul Berger.

III

Oklawaha County Laissez-Faire

10

"ABSORBED IN THE BEAUTY and the ever-changing panorama of the river, I do not wonder that the culmination of his childhood experience came to rest in Oklawaha County," said Jack Rogers. He was speaking to an attentive and reverent crowd at the 1992 Florida Folk Festival in White Springs as part of the Gamble Rogers Memorial Tribute held seven months after his folksinging brother's untimely death.

Jack was recalling a Thanksgiving weekend in 1950 when he and his brother were introduced to the Ocklawaha River in an old handcrafted wooden cruiser purchased by their father two years earlier. "With its curved canopy watery trail winding its way through the Ocala National Forest, we entered into the Ocklawaha at first light, the early morning mist married to the water, and we started an eight-hour trip up an enchanted river to Silver Springs," Jack recalled. Their eyes fixated on the natural beauty that surrounded them, the two boys never moved from the forward cockpit. It was the beginning of a love affair with the Ocklawaha River and provided the inspirational backdrop for the persona of Gamble Rogers the performer and the legacy that was about to unfold.

"He was intensely interested in people, in their thoughts, their fears, and in their hopes," Jack Rogers continued. "He was touched by each of life's experiences, and it surfaced in his work."

After his departure from the Serendipity Singers, the direction of Gamble Roger's professional career was dictated in part by a changing music culture and a changing landscape, especially in his native Florida. By the time he was ready to embark on a solo career, the folk music revolution had for all practical purposes been replaced by Woodstock nation. While there were pockets of folk music still around, the hoote-nanny era seemed like a distant memory.

Lucrative folk gigs were hard to come by, especially for a solo new-comer like Gamble with no professional representation and no hit song to draw the public's attention. His brief tenure with the Seren-dipity Singers had given him some exposure and set him up for a solo tour of major college campuses. But the work was not steady and the crowds were dwindling. The opportunity to make it seemed to have passed him by, so he had little choice but to move back to Florida, where he hoped to reestablish himself and reenergize his folksinging career.

The Florida of the late 1960s was a far cry from the scenic rustic setting where Gamble had grown up in the late 1940s and early 1950s. Central Florida, in particular, was undergoing a major transforma-tion. Cape Canaveral had become the epicenter for the nation's space program. "Used to be the best trout fishing and duck hunting in the Sunshine State," lamented Gamble. "Now it's just cyclone fences, CIA men, and Soviet trawlers."

And sixty miles to the west, land was being bulldozed for a magic kingdom that would soon become the world's best-known vacation destination.

"Disney World, a five-hundred-million-dollar jukebox in the honky tonk of life" is how Gamble would describe it. "The greatest commer-cial concession ever articulated in the entrepreneurial visionings of modern mankind . . . a monument to the legacy of Mickey Mouse."

In the midst of this colossal commercialism, Gamble Rogers re-turned to Florida as a champion of the plain folks and a lover of the state's natural beauty and resources. For a time he settled in Miami's eclectic Coconut Grove community. There he found a vibrant cafe that was still a hotbed for folksingers from around the country. He also teamed up with a new singing partner and romantic interest.

11

~~~~~~~~~~~~~~~~~~~~~~~~~~~~~~~~~~~~

LIFE ON THE ROAD and the pressures to eke out a living as a folksinger had taken its toll on Gamble's personal life by the time he returned to Florida. His marriage to Maggie ended in divorce, and he became romantically and professionally involved with Liz Corrigan, a seasoned folksinger who was also the voice on several TV commercials and jingles.

Elizabeth Seneff was born in Pittsburgh, Pennsylvania, in 1935. Liz was classically trained as a teenager but found her footing in the folk movement in the early 1960s. For a brief period she was a member of the Whiskeyhill Singers, the folk group formed by Dave Guard after he left the Kingston Trio. She released a solo album entitled *Listen to Liz* in 1964 that included the popular "Nobody Knows When You're Down and Out."

Liz took a brief hiatus during her marriage to Robert Corrigan in the mid-1960s but returned to the folk world after their divorce. Her long professional career would include being one of the voices behind "Smile, You're on Candid Camera," the TV show theme song, as well as the jingle for the 1979 "Mean" Joe Greene commercial, "Have a Coke and a Smile." As a solo performer in New York she often closed her shows by thanking the audience and saying, "You know me better than you think." She would then offer a medley of familiar commercials and jingles on which she sang.

Liz and Gamble's venture into the subtropical oasis of Coconut Grove was no surprise. Miami's original bohemian neighborhood, where the jasmine bloomed, was the perfect setting for artists and intellectuals seeking escape from big-city life.

For a nine-year span, from 1964 to 1973, Coconut Grove was home to one of the South's most iconic coffeehouses. The Flick was located on Ponce de Leon Boulevard near the University of Miami campus. It and the Gaslight Lounge, two legendary venues, made Coconut Grove a popular destination for folksingers from around the country.

Billing itself as "Florida's Most Unique Coffee House," the Flick hosted a who's who in North American folk music. Performers included David Crosby, Joni Mitchell, Odetta, Steve Goodman, Jimmy Buffet, John Sebastian, Jerry Jeff Walker, Dion, Vince Martin, Bob Ingram, and Ron Kickasola.

When Gamble took up residence in Coral Gables in the late 1960s, the Flick was a haven, if not a last vestige, for a declining folk scene.

"A booking at the Flick was like having a pension," said Michael Peter Smith, a highly respected singer-songwriter and veteran of the 1960s folk movement. "You went there because no one else was hiring. It was the last club around where you could work six nights a week. It was almost like an island and you were drowning but here was a place you could take up residence."

Smith, a Chicago-based songwriter, is best known for his classic "The Dutchman," popularized by the Irish folksinger Liam Clancy of the Clancy Brothers and later by both Steve Goodman and Gamble Rogers. Smith experienced firsthand the rise and fall of folk's popularity. He recalled,

> In the early '60s when it was prevalent, you didn't even need to advertise who was playing in the coffeehouses. All you needed on your marquee was "Folk Music" or "Hootenanny," and that said it all. It started to die off around 1965 and '66. All the guitar players I knew were considering going electric. It was a natural progression. You started in folk clubs, then you would grow your hair long and pick up an electric guitar. Now it was folk rock.

It was against this backdrop that Smith met Gamble at the Flick. "He could have walked in straight from *Gone with the Wind*," said Smith. "His whole appearance, the way he dressed, even his chin, you knew there was something special."

Smith first heard about Gamble years earlier from a musician friend who had seen Gamble and Champion during their years at the Baffled Knight in Tallahassee. "He couldn't stop talking about him," Smith said.

Smith's initial impression at the Flick was that Gamble was one of the best guitar players he had ever seen. But there was more to Gamble's performance. His brief stint with the Serendipity Singers had convinced Gamble that the stage banter that went on between songs was a key to keeping the audiences attentive.

"Humor had to be added to the repertoire," said Smith. "We were all doing what we needed to do." In certain ways, Rogers's performances were akin to a one-man variety show, with the musician playing the dual role of folksinger and jester. Telling stories between songs had always been a part of the folk tradition. It was now becoming an art form in and of itself, born out of necessity to keep folk music alive and the audiences engaged.

Gamble's first efforts at storytelling were limited to humorous anecdotes about people and places he experienced either on the farm in the Nacoochee Valley or during his high school days in Winter Park. Slowly, fictionalized characters began to emerge and the stories were embellished.

One of the first characters he developed was Agamemnon Abromovitz, a rural entrepreneur who dabbled in the chicken and cattle businesses. In a recorded performance at the Flick in 1971, Gamble, quietly strumming chords in the background, spoke softly of the deceased Agamemnon: "His wife, Elfrieda, had his ashes scattered over his favorite catfish hole on the Chattahoochee River. She saved enough of his ashes to fill a tiny hourglass. Keeps it on the back of the stove. Uses it for an egg timer. She always said that even at his best, Agamemnon was never good for more than three minutes."

Gamble then called, "Look out, now" and went straight into a mesmerizing guitar-picking solo that wowed the crowd. It was the beginnings of an act that would soon set Gamble apart as a performer. His preacherlike delivery, timing, and connectivity with an audience were literally being played out on the stages of the Flick and other stops along the Florida coffeehouse circuit.

While the storytelling may have been a little rough around the edges, Gamble's guitar picking had few equals. His onstage charisma was hard to overlook.

"He was a traditional southern gentleman, and you could see that on the stage right away," said Michael Peter Smith. "He didn't need to pick up a guitar to get that kind of response from people. You automatically had a certain respect for him. He had a physical presence that was very charming. You could put a suit on him and take him anywhere. He had a great profile and a great jaw."

When they performed together, Gamble Rogers and Liz Corrigan were a powerful duo. "I recently saw a photo of Liz singing with Gamble," said Smith. "They were gorgeous. I realize now what the impact must have been back then."

Gamble's and Smith's paths crossed again when Gamble began performing Smith's "The Dutchman" in the mid-1970s. It became a signature song for Gamble and inextricably linked the two performers.

At the Flick, Gamble performed alongside some of the legends of folk music carving out his own niche and professional identity. Between gigs in Coconut Grove, he took his evolving act to less-known clubs and coffeehouses in St. Augustine, Tallahassee, and Gainesville. He met up with some old friends and picked up a whole new cast of characters along the way.

12

~~~~~~~~~~~~~~~~~~~~~~~~~~

What a funky place the Tradewinds is, what memories are summoned up.

—GAMBLE ROGERS, JACKSONVILLE CIVIC AUDITORIUM, 1976

BOB PATTERSON HAD NO IDEA the tap on shoulder would transform his life.

"Howdy, howdy, howdy. I'm Gamble Rogers and this is my friend Will McLean and we're fellow guitar players" is the greeting Patterson received." The scene was at the bar at Tradewinds Tropical Lounge in the heart of downtown St. Augustine, where a lively crowd of patrons and area musicians was engaged in a nightly routine of one-upsmanship.

Less than twenty-four hours earlier, Patterson was camped out alone on nearby Conch Island with little more than his twelve-string guitar. In the mid-1960s, while Gamble Rogers was touring college campuses with the Serendipity Singers, Patterson was playing rhythm guitar and singing vocals for a psychedelic rock band called Elizabeth. The band had a hit song, "Mary Anne," and is featured on a viral You Tube video as one of the "Fifty Psychedelic '60s Bands to Hear Before You Die."

By the time he arrived in Florida and was camping out on Conch Island, Patterson was pretty much out of money and searching for a bar or tavern where he might land a gig. He found that and a lot more at the notorious Tradewinds.

Billed as "the Oldest Lounge in the Oldest City," the Tradewinds Tropical Lounge has a rich and storied history. Founded by two merchant marine sailors, the bar opened in 1945 as the South Seas Lounge.

Through several ownership and name changes, the Tradewinds developed its reputation as the popular port of call in the early 1960s under the ownership of Walter "Duke" Leonard and his wife, Toni. Known as much for its patrons and decor as the food and music, the Tradewinds could offer as unpredictable and stormy a night as the tropical Florida weather.

"The Tradewinds was an amazing place, right out of a Hemingway novel, because it was so loaded with outrageous characters all involved in trying to outdo each other in who could be the most outrageous," said Patterson.

Among the most outrageous was North Florida's own Art Schill, an original member of the Folksters musical trio who was known for his outlandish antics and off-color comedy routines at the Tradewinds. "He would arrive in a hearse, get up on stage in Don Rickles fashion, and just assassinate the audience," remembered Patterson. In the audience was an eclectic mix of doctors, lawyers, and bankers alongside shrimpers, rednecks, and rough and tough townies. Everybody seemed to gather at the pub on Charlotte Street with the bamboo decor.

Patterson recalled his first night at the Tradewinds:

> From the street outside I could hear the sound of a banjo being played as good as anybody could play a banjo. On stage was Paul Champion and Jim Ballew. I walked in with my twelve-string and took a seat at the bar and ordered a drink from a short, stubby bartender with a handlebar mustache named Waxy. The two owners, Duke and Toni, came over and asked me to do a guest set. They had just had a cancellation and offered me a gig six nights a week for the next six weeks. I never knew that first night would have so much meaning.

Patterson also didn't know that his introduction to Gamble Rogers that first night would be the beginning of a transformational friendship.

Gamble traveled from Coconut Grove, where he had been playing at the Flick. From the beginning Patterson sensed he and Gamble were kindred spirits living parallel lives. "We were both kind of the black sheep of our families. Both of us had played in bands, we were both divorced and paying child support, and we both shared the ethics of a Boy Scout. But we had also both tripped that switch, that we were going to write songs and play music. We had made that deal just like Robert Johnson at the crossroads." Johnson was the legendary bluesman who, according to folklore, sold his soul to the devil for a lifetime of easy money, women, and fame.

For a time after they met, Patterson, along with bass player Don Smith, backed up Gamble at the Tradewinds whenever he would come up to St. Augustine from Coconut Grove. What they witnessed was the emergence of a star.

"Saturday nights at the Tradewinds would be packed," Patterson remembered. "We'd be up there on stage playing our asses off and there ain't nobody listening. So here enters Gamble and the real value of storytelling."

He added, "We had all used little stories as introductions to songs from day one. But Gamble had the realization the stories could stand by themselves. They didn't need to be just introductions. So that was the seed. I watched it grow over the period."

If there was ever a venue that could challenge a performer to push the limits of the entertainment envelope it was the rowdy and raucous Tradewinds. "There would be nights we would worry about our safety, although as performers we felt like we had some kind of diplomatic immunity," Patterson said.

In the midst of the tumult, Gamble would get on stage and over time win the audience over with his demeanor, his charm, and his talent.

"The amazing thing about Gamble was his ability to make people laugh," said Patterson. "And I'm not talking about just laughter, he'd make them lose it. He got to the point where he'd be doing his show and just by the gesture of his hand or the way he turned his body he would make people roll over in their chairs."

The audiences were not always immediately impressed. "There would be tables of people who didn't care for him at all," Patterson recalled. "And there would be some people who might even want to punch him out for some of the things he said. But at the end of the night, those same people walked away loving Gamble. It was amazing to be a witness to that."

Whenever he was in town, the locals would come back to hear the same stories. Gamble used the opportunity to tweak the characters and tales by paying close attention to the audience response.

Gamble could take a single incident like being issued a warning citation by a state trooper in DeKalb County, Georgia, and turn it into a five-minute commentary on southern culture.

> Now I could tell by the clothes he was wearing that this deputy was some kind of a primitive man. He had on a breechclout made out of two Fruehauf mud flaps. He had a styrofoam pith helmet with an STP decal on the front, Thom McAn penny loafers with quarters stuck in the top. And he was well armed in the tradition of the North Georgia law. Over his bare chest he had two .45 calibre bandolier belts with cartridge loops alternately stuffed with Hav-A-Tampa Jewels and Slim Jims. Had a shoulder holster made out of a PF sneaker with a toe cut out, carrying an axe handle personally autographed by Lester Maddox. . . . Now in DeKalb County, Georgia, those warning citations are printed up in the form of bumper stickers. He went back to his tractor, got me a citation, peeled the brown paper off the back, licked it one time, slopped it over the back of my automobile. I went back and read it later on. It said, "Eat More Possum."

Years after he began telling that story, Gamble was presented a certificate naming him an honorary deputy sheriff of Dekalb County, Georgia.

"I'll tell you after twenty years in this business that's the finest honor I've ever been given," Gamble told a crowd at the 1987 Florida Folk Festival. "I've got that certificate at home on the wall, framed. The same way they framed me in DeKalb County in 1970."

Whether at the Tradewinds or a larger outdoor music festival, Gamble never wasted a moment on stage. The simple task of tuning his guitar between songs presented the opportunity for a humorous interlude. "This is the last guitar I'll ever buy at a Stuckey's stand," he said, referring to the roadside convenience and candy store chain that dotted the Southeast in the 1960s. "Yes ma'am. See those inlays? Honey nougat and praline. Hard times don't scare me none. If I can't pick for a living I'll just eat this thing."

It wasn't long before Gamble became a top draw at the Tradewinds. It was the perfect setting for him to hone his craft. As his reputation grew, so too did his sphere of influence. At the Tradewinds, Gamble became much more than an entertainer. He was a mentor, a role model, and often a peacemaker.

Bruce McEwan, Gamble's childhood friend, remembered the night he took his cousin to hear Gamble at the Tradewinds. A local male florist started putting a move on McEwan. "He was pretty drunk, and I kept elbowing him and pushing him away," said McEwan. "Finally we took our issues outside the bar and I was ready to punch him out. Gamble saw the whole thing unfold on stage. He put his guitar down in the middle of his show, came outside, and in a quiet voice calmed us both down." There were no punches thrown.

Gamble's command and presence were never more evident than at the Tradewinds' legendary Palm Sunday shows. "It wasn't the kind of place you'd want to take your kids," said Gamble's brother, Jack. In other words, it wasn't your typical church crowd.

Folksinger Jim Carrick elaborated on the scene.

On Palm Sunday, there would be absolute chaos in there, people slinging beer all over the place, women taking their tops off. In walks Gamble on stage. Now there's two schools of thought on how to handle a rowdy crowd. You can play louder or you can play softer. Gamble would walk up there and start to play so soft you could hardly hear him. He'd look around the room. The crowd would eventually start to hear this beautiful sound, and before you knew it you could hear a pin drop. He owned every one of them. Now that's a real gift.

It was as if the whole texture of the room changed once he got on stage. "They might not have even known who he was, but they knew he was somebody by the way he carried himself," recalled Carrick.

Aspiring musicians would come to the Tradewinds just to study Gamble's performance and maybe pick up a lick or two.

Charley Simmons was a young up-and-coming guitar picker from Delaware who began playing the six-string when he was nine years old. In 1970 he moved to St. Augustine, where his exposure to Gamble Rogers changed his whole approach to guitar playing.

"Whenever Gamble was in town, I'd go over to the Tradewinds, sit by the stage, and study Gamble's every move," Simmons recalled. This routine went on for almost two years. "One night, Gamble comes over to the side of the stage, hands me his guitar, and says, 'OK, let me see what you've got.'" After Simmons played, Gamble told him, "You didn't have to steal any of these licks. I would have just given them to you."

Simmons began to emulate Rogers's style of guitar playing and became the 1992 Utah State Flattop Guitar Champion and the 2002 Wyoming State Finger Style Champion. He wrote a moving tribute, "Song for Gamble," and is considered around St. Augustine as the one who comes closest to picking the guitar like Gamble.

While Gamble eventually took his solo act to taverns and stages across North America, he always returned to the Tradewinds. It was where he ruled the roost. He was the club's ambassador and unofficial booking agent. He used the Tradewinds to help his fledgling friends like Jimmy Buffett get some exposure on their way to the big time. And he assisted in bringing legends like Odetta and Doc Watson to the Charlotte Street pub.

At a June 27, 1976, concert at the Jacksonville Civic Auditorium as he was opening for the Earl Scruggs Revue, Gamble offered the audience his own description of the bawdy Tradewinds.

A typical Tradewinds Saturday night, all them good ol' boys stuffed in there like anchovies in a pressure cooker kicking ass . . . a turgid purple lamination of smoke clings to the ceiling and shimmering down the midnight air a hundred thousand hapless, helpless, misdirected assignations dangling like declensions of despair. And through the front door curls a tongue of smoke which splits itself about the flag pole in front of the American Legion Hall only to merge with the salt sea air and the pigeon droppings on Cathedral Street.

Most believe it was the Tradewinds that served in part as a real-life model for Gamble's most notorious and iconic locale in his fictitious Oklawaha County, the Terminal Tavern. "A skull orchard, a temple of culture, and a taproot to certain wellsprings of human behavior" is how Gamble described the Terminal Tavern. Much like the Tradewinds, the

Terminal Tavern's patrons were a "raffish clientele made up of grape-fruit wine drinkers, trotline rustlers, pool hall hustlers, dirt road sports, garden variety scofflaws, genteel schizophrenics, and good ol' girls."

The perfect platform from which to be anointed Troubadour Emeritus.

13

~~~~~~~~~~~~~~~~

For the Ancient City is a place of artists and writers, as well as fools and fishermen.

—Gamble Rogers, introduction to "Doris"

It was no accident that Gamble Rogers, who had been living and performing in Coconut Grove, eventually established a permanent residence in the ancient city of St. Augustine, Florida. Founded in 1565, fifty-five years before the pilgrims landed at Plymouth Rock, St. Augustine is the oldest continuously occupied European settlement on the North American continent. The magical seaside community has at one time or another been home to Native Americans, Spanish explorers, British soldiers, artists, pirates, fishermen, and business tycoons. Much of the city's culture and history is preserved within the remnants of its coquina walls and cobblestone streets, rumored to be inhabited by ghosts and apparitions assigned to protect its ancient secrets and treasures. St. Augustine has long been a haven for aspiring artists and musicians who hover in the city's narrow streets and bring life to its many eclectic galleries and cafes.

As a child, Gamble's mother, Evelyn, wintered in St. Augustine with her family. As an adult, she returned with her own young children in tow to visit new sites like Marineland, to the south, as well as the city's historical standards like the Old Jail and Castillo de San Marcos, the fort built by Spaniards in the late 1600s.

In many ways St. Augustine remained a throwback to the Old Florida Gamble had come to love as a child. His was a childhood spent exploring Florida's natural beauty and wildlife as yet untarnished by the commercialism on the horizon. Gamble's daughter Lyn witnessed firsthand the clash of being raised by her father in the new Florida of the 1970s, with its glut of hotel chains and theme parks that were taking over Central Florida. Walt Disney World was among Gamble's favorite targets and the subject of some of his most biting satire. "I remember asking him once, somewhat hurt that he would poke fun at such an icon, as to why he hated Disney World so much," Lyn said.

"It's not that I hate Disney World," he told her. "It's just that they took away the best duck hunting in the Southeast." The robotic Jungle Cruise attraction at the Magic Kingdom bore little resemblance to the real alligator hunting he had done with his Boy Scout troop back in Winter Park.

On the other hand, the Ancient City provided Gamble a welcome return to earlier times and a circle of friends who shared his love of music and carried with them a certain air of authenticity.

The late 1960s and early 1970s attracted a unique cast of characters who either lived nearby or were frequent visitors to downtown St. Augustine. Among them were some of Gamble's old pals and picking partners like Paul Champion, Jim Ballew, and Will McLean. There were new friendships forged as well with Bob Patterson, Charlie Robertson, Daryl Wise, Don Dunaway, Jim Carrick, and others.

"There was an almost mystical atmosphere here," remembered Carrick. "It was carefree. Nobody was making any money, but nobody cared. The streets were just filled with music. It was a special time."

Carrick was a young, aspiring guitar player in Jacksonville when he met Gamble Rogers at the Fernandina Shrimp Festival in the early 1970s. "I was just blown away by his guitar playing," Carrick remembered. "It changed everything for me."

It wasn't long before Carrick became a Rogers groupie, following him around the state to soak up anything he could learn and cherishing every moment he could spend with his newfound folk hero.

"I followed him everywhere," Carrick said. "I just kept showing up. He was always so gracious." Instead of taking a break during his performances, Gamble would pull up a chair and hand Carrick his custom-made Randy Wood guitar. He'd go back and forth with his young apprentice, teaching him the guitar-picking technique he had just performed on stage. "He just had this way of moving right in with a person because he was very interested in you. He learned from people. Here I was, just this wet-nosed kid, but he was learning from me, too."

Whenever Gamble played the Tradewinds in St. Augustine, Carrick was there. If Gamble was playing a six-night stint, Carrick would be there every night even though he was underage. After a performance, Carrick often phoned Gamble and asked him how to play a particular chord or lick. Their friendship continued through the years with countless nights of jamming at Gamble's St. Augustine home following a dinner featuring the folk singer's homemade collard greens, a Carrick favorite.

What Carrick and others soon found out was that a friendship with Gamble transcended most other relationships. "He was an example of someone who lived in the truth," Carrick said. "He gave me a sense of morality I didn't have before. Not only did he teach us how to play music, but he taught us how to conduct ourselves during the time in between playing the music."

In 1987 Carrick hit a low time in his life. His wife had left him, he had lost interest in a business he owned in Ponte Vedra Beach, and he was still feeling the emotional effect of having lost a child to a miscarriage when, seemingly out of nowhere, the phone rang. "Jiiiim, it's Gaaamble," said the clearly identifiable voice on the other end. Rogers had just finished playing a show in the Northeast. He asked Carrick to meet him at the Daytona airport, where he had parked his car. For the next week, Gamble and Carrick traveled around the state in an old diesel Mercedes. "You couldn't go over sixty miles per hour because it was sure to overheat," Carrick said. Carrick handled sound for Gamble as he played a few local gigs, and they spent hours together just hanging out and playing guitar.

"The remarkable thing was, we never once talked about my problems," Carrick reflected. At the end of the trip, Gamble took Carrick down to Wekiwa Springs and rented a canoe. "This is what I do when I've got trouble," Gamble said.

He left Carrick alone with the canoe and said he'd be back for him in a couple of hours. "He knew just what I needed," Carrick said. "He gave me the space and the time to think it all through. Most of us have to work at being the good guy. To Gamble, it just came naturally."

Charlie Robertson was another of St. Augustine's celebrated characters who fell into Gamble's musical orbit. His unique brand of songwriting, with titles like "Life in Parentheses" and "Dalai Lama's Birthday," eventually cast him into the upper tier of Gamble's favorite songwriters.

"Charlie Robertson is God's personal songwriter," Gamble once proclaimed. Robertson took such tributes in stride, with his typical self-deprecating humility.

"That's one of the things you long for, and when it comes out it's embarrassing," Robertson said of Rogers's compliment. "I'd characterize it as Lawrence Olivier asking Pauly Shore for acting tips."

Robertson met Gamble at a picking party held at a Northeast Florida fish camp in 1968. "I had written a few songs myself and thought I was pretty damn good," Robertson remembered. Then he heard Gamble's "The Girl from Stoney Lonesome" and realized how high the songwriting bar had been raised.

"It was typical of the kind of stuff he wrote back then," said Robertson. "You could see the Faulkner influence. It was this beautiful bucolic-sounding song that evolved into a classic southern murder ballad with much better guitar and way better lyrics than you were used to."

Oh the green Ohio River, the Wabash, and the Mississippi flood
Carried her to Memphis on a Sunday, but Monday was the message
   in her blood.

                              Gamble Rogers, "The Girl from Stoney Lonesome"

As a songwriter, Robertson said he knew right then he wasn't ready to sit at the table with the grownups just yet. The two struck up a friendship during Gamble's early years in St. Augustine when he was living at the Seabreeze Court and dining regularly at O'Steen's Restaurant. St. Augustine and the Tradewinds Tropical Lounge in particular had become Gamble's boot camp. "That's where he worked out all of his stories so that when he went to the so-called quality listening venues he was as hard as a Marine," said Robertson.

"Gamble inserted himself in my life without being asked and helped me upgrade my musical orbit, which is about the same thing he did for everyone I knew," Robertson acknowledged. As the years passed and Gamble became better known as a performer, he took his friends along with him, opening doors and providing opportunities.

"I didn't know I was this good, but Gamble would say this club needs to hear you. Suddenly I was playing places like the Last Resort in Athens, Georgia, the Exit Inn in Nashville, and Earl of Old Town in Chicago," Robertson said.

Robertson was among those invited to join a musical revue Gamble assembled known as Cassadaga Stories. Cassadaga is a small community in Volusia County, Florida, known for its population of psychics and mediums. It is sometimes referred to as "the Psychic Capital of the World." Cassadaga Stories included Gamble's friends Paul Champion, Will McLean, Jim Ballew, Bob Patterson, Don Smith, Liz Corrigan, Terri Desire, and eventually Charlie Robertson. Together they would tour college campuses for four-hour concerts, during which each of the performers would have his or her own spot.

While still a powerful singing duo, Gamble and Liz were nearing the end of their up-and-down romance not long after Gamble moved to St. Augustine. "That was an interesting relationship," remembered Robertson. "They were on the downslide. There was a fiery love there, but there was a war zone, too."

Bob Patterson observed that Gamble and Liz had their good times and their difficulties.

"You have to realize we were all a bunch of young guys, guitar pickers," Patterson said. "Gamble had a lot of women hitting on him. I guess we all did. Maybe that's one of the reasons we picked up the guitar in the first place. There was a lot of that going on. We always thought as we drove around the state that we were going to die as we were being shot in the back by some jealous husband."

In the midst of it all, it came as a surprise to Robertson that Gamble's background seemed to have so little in common with the band of followers who had come to revere him. "What I learned is that Gamble had thrown himself into this maelstrom that was not his natural habitat, and the people he took an interest in were far off his radar. People like Will McLean and Paul Champion were nothing like the people he had grown up with," Robertson said.

Even the way he came about his music was different, Robertson said. "As accomplished as he was, he was by no means a natural musician. It was his architecture background that kicked in. He took the music and songwriting from the foundation up and applied his own aesthetic." Robertson recognized the clear influence of Gamble's father, the renowned Florida architect. "The aesthetics of his father combined these arcane elements with a kind of ultrasophistication. It was like going from Shakespeare to Hank Williams without a hitch."

Robertson acknowledged that Gamble's parents were not totally pleased with his decision to spurn architecture for a career as a folksinger. "It was as if they'd put him through three years with the Alvin Ailey Dance Troupe and he was out there working as a pole dancer. They just didn't get it at first," he said. "They did have an appreciation, though, of the cross-pollination of the work ethic, and they realized how much it mattered to him, that he wanted to do something that was his own."

For Robertson and others, Gamble emerged as the go-to guy among his peers and proteges. If you had a new song, you ran it by Gamble first. Always the diplomat, he might suggest an alternative way of doing things, careful to not be overly critical.

For his part, Robertson made his own contribution to Gamble's legacy. Robertson, a Vietnam-era draftee, had a friend during the Vietnam War who was a conscientious objector doing public service as an orderly at a psychiatric ward near downtown Orlando. After a visit one evening, Robertson and his friend walked home together after the late-night shift change.

"We walked past this terrible-looking Trailways bus station, and next to it was an even more terrible-looking bar called the Terminal Tavern," said Robertson. "It just struck me as being metaphysically hilarious.

You can't dangle something like that in front of a writer and not expect to suck it right up like a Hoover."

Robertson returned to where he was serving at an Army post in Kansas and wrote a surrealistic song he titled "The Devil Took Miami," based on a bar called the Terminal Tavern. Gamble heard the song and asked Robertson if he could use the Terminal Tavern. Flattered at the request, Robertson obliged.

Of the many other personal relationships Gamble forged over the years, none would be as important or influential as the friendship he developed with Will McLean, the Black Hat Troubadour and the father of Florida folk music.

14

AT THE 1982 FLORIDA FOLK FESTIVAL in White Springs, Gamble Rogers began slowly picking the introductory notes to "The Orange Blossom Special" when he began to reminisce.

"It was exactly twenty years ago that I came to Tallahassee with Paul Champion and Chuck Glore and started a little coffeehouse on North Adams Street," he said, referring to the Baffled Knight. "One of the people who blew in through the door was somebody who changed my life by the example of his music and the way he lived his life."

He went on to introduce Will McLean, the father of Florida folk music. Together, Gamble Rogers and Will McLean played hundreds of shows and spent countless hours cavorting around Florida swapping songs and telling stories.

It was McLean who helped instill in Gamble a cause with which he was already predisposed—a love of Florida and its natural beauty. Born in Chipley, Florida, in 1919, McLean early on acquired an appreciation for Florida's pristine and primitive backwoods and the wildlife that roamed the land. He detested land developers and big business for raping the native soil in the name of progress.

A patriot at heart, McLean served his country by enlisting in the Air Force during World War II. He was shot down over the Pacific and held as a prisoner of war. Legend has it that he escaped from a bamboo cage using only his teeth and his sheer determination.

When he returned to Florida after the war, McLean embarked on his life's mission, to rescue Florida from the ravages of the uncontrolled commercial development he sensed was destroying the state's natural beauty and resources. His weapon was his guitar and his voice, and he sang of his own personal connections in songs like "My Soul Is a Hawk." He brought color and life to Florida's culture and history with ballads like "Tate's Hell" and "Osceola's Last Words," and he championed the cause of conservationists with his prayerful "Lord Hold Back the Waters of Lake Okeechobee."

A man of few possessions, McLean lived the life of a drifter. He was a chain smoker and a notorious drinker. No one, it seemed, could outdrink Will McLean. During his periods of intoxication, which were frequent, McLean had a penchant for giving away what few possessions he owned.

The luthier Paul Berger remembered the time McLean drifted into his St. Augustine shop wanting to borrow a guitar. "So I called Gamble to see what he thought," recalled Berger.

"Well, you know Will's a good friend," Gamble told Berger. "But he does get to drinking now and then, and if that happens, he might just give that guitar away." Berger heeded the warning but lent the guitar to McLean, who did return it several days later.

Despite his sometimes careless and carefree lifestyle, there was no denying McLean's ubiquitous influence as a crusader and torch bearer for his native state.

"Will's stories were magical, and they really resonated with Gamble," said Bob Patterson. "You just knew there was something special about him."

For Gamble, McLean was a mentor and an inspiration who deepened his own appreciation and love for Florida. For McLean, Gamble was a new voice who shared his vision and values. He was also McLean's ticket out of jail, bailing him out and posting his bond on several occasions.

McLean and Rogers performed together at saloons and festivals around the state. Wherever they performed, it seemed they always found time to return to St. Augustine and the Tradewinds Tropical Lounge.

Jim Carrick remembered how Gamble, true to form, would offer up an eloquent and effusive introduction of McLean as only Gamble could, to which McLean would respond, "Oh, Gamble, I ain't nothin' but a country boy with a big belly and a little peenie."

For all of his public image, McLean was a complex and deep thinker whom Gamble admired deeply. In a eulogy Gamble recited upon McLean's death in 1990, he said, "Will McLean knew that what truly separates man from the animals is the capacity for the human heart to stand divided against itself. Time and again he bore this conflict up to us bravely and shone before us his nakedness. Often we thought this humbled him, when it was we ourselves who should have been humbled."

Standing tall among the other Florida environmentalists turned folksingers who were among Gamble's early inner circle was Dale "Spider" Crider. A basketball player for the University of Missouri, Crider moved to Florida after college and was hired by the state as an Everglades biologist.

"You can only play basketball for so long," Crider said. He spent a few years flying over the Everglades doing aerial surveys of the Florida wetlands before moving to Gainesville, where he began a thirty-year distinguished career with the Florida Game and Fresh Water Fish Commission as a waterfowl biologist and education specialist.

Crider said he met Gamble and McLean at the 1963 Florida Folk Festival in White Springs. It was there that Crider decided he could combine his passion for the environment with his interest in music. Lincolnesque in stature and quirky by nature, Crider wrote a collection of songs dedicated to the preservation of Florida's wildlife and fragile aquatic ecosystems. Among his most popular songs are "I'm the Mangrove Buccaneer" and "Apalachicola Doin' Time."

When Gamble came to Gainesville to perform, he often hooked up with Crider at Anhinga Roost, Crider's Shrek-like rural homestead on Newnans Lake not far from the University of Florida campus. Crider's residence was a popular hangout for Gamble's friends like McLean, Don Grooms, and others.

On one particular evening, Gamble was booked for a show at Gainesville's Beef 'n Bottle Lounge. He invited Crider to come along, but Crider declined because he was in charge of looking after his four-year-old son, Hunter.

"Oh bring him along," Gamble said. "He'll enjoy the show."

Shortly after arriving at the Beef 'n Bottle, Hunter fell asleep. "I just laid him up in the balcony," recalled Crider. "When Gamble finished the show we got in the car and took off. We were almost back at my home when I realized *Oh damn, we left Hunter back at the bar!* Well, Gamble turned that ol' lime green Mustang around so fast and we headed back to the bar."

The janitor who was cleaning up after hours didn't want to let the two men back inside. "We rapped and rapped on the door and he kept telling us he was closed," said Crider. "Gamble told him who he was, but this janitor didn't know Gamble Rogers. He finally cracked the door enough that I was able to sneak through and run right by him over to the balcony. There was Hunter, still asleep. I didn't think it was too funny at the time."

The incident would be chronicled by Jacksonville musician Larry Mangum in his "Ballad of Dale and Gamble."

> Don't leave the kids with a picker, there's a guitar in the house.
> You might as well leave 'em standing in the road.
> They'll pretend to be listening when you tell them what to do,
> But the truth is all musicians are addicted to the muse.
> You can trust them with the yard work and they can make a pretty
>   good spouse.
> Don't leave the kids with a picker, there's a guitar in the house.

The characters with whom Gamble associated, their commitment to the folk tradition, and the causes that inspired their art all converged in and around St. Augustine in the late 1960s and early 1970s, making it a special time in a special place.

"We as human beings have an innate desire to be a part of something," said Gamble's close friend Bob Patterson. "We all belonged to a group of guitar players, singing songs and telling stories, who bonded over protecting what was happening to Florida, and it resonated with all of us. Without that, this story never happens." Add to it the magic and wonder of St. Augustine. "At the time, this was the nucleus, the energy source that Gamble used to step out."

15

WHILE GAMBLE WAS RAPIDLY DEVELOPING a loyal and closeknit following in his native state, he was still without much commercial success and generating little money from his folksinging career. It wasn't for lack of effort.

His schedule was grueling. In addition to his regular Florida circuit of coffeehouses and folk festivals Gamble was hitting the road hard, picking up gigs anywhere he could land them. Roadside bars, college towns, and big cities like Chicago and Detroit were on his makeshift itinerary.

He was virtually living out of a suitcase, staying at cheap motels, and racking up untold mileage on his 1965 lime green Mustang he named "the Green Jesus." The car was a classic, retrofitted with larger seats to accommodate his deteriorating back condition.

The back seat was often littered with empty buckets of Kentucky Fried Chicken and sweet tea cups that covered his guitar case. More than sheer economics, Gamble much preferred the solitude of his beat-up automobile over flying. His hours behind the wheel of the Green Jesus gave him ample time to rehearse and perfect the depth and character of his stories, which were becoming more a part of his onstage repertoire.

With his rich southern drawl and dressed in wrinkled Levi's and a denim shirt with pearl snap buttons, Gamble must have appeared as pure hillbilly to those unfamiliar with his act or his educated background. But once on stage there was no doubting his talent as a masterful guitar player and raconteur with a gifted command of the English language.

While he may not have harbored any grand illusions of commercial greatness, there were still bills to pay, including child support back in Florida. Making ends meet was a challenge.

"Those first long trips, whenever he'd go to Chicago or Michigan, it would cost him more than he would make," said Patterson.

In a 1974 interview with Associated Press writer Evelyn August, Gamble seemed content and encouraged that his career was on the upswing. Interviewed at a nine dollar a night Detroit hotel room, Gamble acknowledged he was on the road ten months a year and had piled up 177,000 miles on his "super charged clunker."

"I seem to be on the verge of commercial success," said Gamble. "I'm working for good people. I have an audience. A person who does what I do can't ask for anything more than that."

Part of Gamble's optimism was linked to his relationship with Nashville's Chuck Glaser, who became Gamble's first professional manager in late 1973. Glaser was part of the popular Nashville country trio Tompall and the Glaser Brothers, who turned their musical talents and influence into Glaser Sound Studios in the early 1970s. The Glasers were major figures in country music's outlaw movement.

Chuck Glaser was predicting big things for Gamble. He told August of the Associated Press that Gamble was on the verge of "hitting it big" and was not only on his way to doubling his income but stood poised to potentially make five times more than the previous year, when he was on his own.

However, Glaser Sound Studios, commonly referred to as Hillbilly Central, had bigger names in its stable, like Waylon Jennings, Kris Kristofferson, and Kinky Friedman. With all that star power, it became increasingly evident that Glaser would simply not have the time to propel Gamble's career to meet what seemed to be very high expectations. Undeterred, Gamble continued to plow ahead, traveling the country in the Green Jesus, always returning to Florida, where his grassroots following and popularity were continuing to grow.

It was back in Florida, while performing at Gainesville's Rathskellar, that Gamble would find someone with the time, dedication, and skill to take his career to the next level. Like Gamble, Charles Steadham abandoned college just short of graduation to pursue his own music passions, which were very different from the folksinger he would soon come to represent.

Steadham was a promising student when he enrolled at the University of Florida in 1962 in pursuit of an accounting degree. He found himself smitten with sounds of the rhythm and blues and jazz he was hearing from young black musicians jamming four nights a week at a club called Sarah's. "The emotion of that music spoke to me," Steadham recalled. One trimester short of an accounting degree, Steadham dropped out to pursue his musical interests. "I entered with a 4.0 and exited with a 1.99," he said.

He was motivated in part by his friendship with a white female vocalist, Linda Lyndell, who he recalled could "sing with real heartfelt passion." Together they played with a variety of rhythm and blues bands that traveled the South's chitlin' circuit during the dark days of segregation. While it was a safe haven for the black performers, Steadham found it necessary to alter his appearance for his own safety.

"It was really a novelty for anyone Caucasian to play in those bands," Steadham said. "It was very important to be discreet." As a result, he donned an Afro wig and dark sunglasses so he could pass as a light-skinned African American. He adopted the stage name Charlie Blade and carried a British commander boot knife strapped to his leg.

Steadham eventually became the booking agent for his own band. "I couldn't find an honest agent to represent us," he said. It wasn't long before the segregation tide began to turn and having an integrated band became an asset rather than a liability, especially on military bases and college campuses. If his own group wasn't available for a particular gig, Steadham used his familiarity with the venue and other bands to offer an alternative. He began to see a future in booking other entertainers and formed the Blade Agency in Gainesville in 1974.

Among the lessons that Steadham learned early on as a booking agent was that all bands, including his own, eventually split up. "The drummer will run off with the guitar player's girlfriend or someone will get arrested," Steadham said. "Some chapter of human drama will unfold and bands will break up. So I began looking for solo acts that you could invest time in and not have it all disintegrate six months later with some domestic dispute."

Steadham's younger brother had been managing UF's Rathskellar, the medieval-themed parlor that was the first campus venue to serve beer. "He told me about this incredible, funny, entertaining singer-songwriter that kept coming into the Rathskellar and just packed the place and had people on the floor with laughter," Steadham said. "He begged me to come hear this fellow named Gamble Rogers, so I did one night and was just mesmerized."

Steadham always liked to watch an act from the back of the room so he could asses the crowd's reaction. "Gamble had them in the palm of his hand," Steadham recalled.

After the performance, Steadham introduced himself. "You couldn't meet Gamble and not like him, with his demeanor, his poise, and his gracious, soft-spoken manner."

Gamble was still working for Chuck Glaser at the time, but the predictions of increasing his income fivefold had yet to materialize. "Chuck had his hands full with the likes of Waylon Jennings and the Outlaws," Steadham said. "He didn't have time for little ol' Gamble. Chuck was doing the best he could, but he just didn't have enough time."

Building a singer's career was a huge endeavor, especially trying to do so from Nashville. It almost seemed as if it required filling up an entire building with a staff whose sole purpose was to promote a single career.

A handshake arrangement was all Steadham needed to start representing Gamble full time. There was never a formal agreement. "I knew immediately that if Gamble told me something, I could believe it," Steadham said.

Steadham's primary goal was to get Gamble a better payday for his life's work. With the singer's consent, he built on what was already a demanding and zealous travel schedule of about 225 dates a year. Gamble loved to perform, but it took its toll on his personal life and his ailing back. Steadham referred to it as "beating your head against the asphalt."

Having Steadham on board to handle the business side was a major relief. Gamble now had a full-time advocate attending to details of his booking contracts and negotiating his performance fees, something that didn't necessarily come naturally to the singer song-writer. "As much as he understood the business side, he was never motivated by money," Steadham said. "If anything, he was conflicted by success."

Whether the performance fee was $500 one night or $2,000 the next, Gamble didn't seem to care. He put the same energy into every show. It was not unheard of for him to refuse his fee if attendance was lacking at a particular venue.

His heavy travel schedule was challenging. To make matters worse, Gamble steadfastly refused to carry a credit card. In his stories he took frequent jabs at the "cosmic consumer" and poked fun at banks and credit ratings. His "Cape Canaveral Talking Blues" is an example.

> We live in a consumer economy, which means basically, the only way any of us can have a credit rating is that we have to show an ability to handle debt. That's the gross side of the national product.

Gamble wanted to pay as he went and didn't believe in getting behind with the banks, Steadham said.

Another challenge was that Gamble's act didn't exactly conform to mainstream media. His hilarious but lengthy front-porch monologues depicting the more colorful side of southern life didn't lend themselves to a three-minute slot on *The Tonight Show*, recalled Steadham.

A case in point was Gamble's late-career audition for a spot on the *New Smothers Brothers Comedy Hour*, a 1980s revival of the duo's 1960s variety show. The audition was arranged by Jim Stafford, one of the show's regulars and the program's writing supervisor. Gamble and Stafford were good friends who had crossed paths in their early days as entertainers. "We played a lot of the same places but seemed to miss each other," Stafford recalled, "although I played more of the places that served booze."

Joining Gamble for the audition was Mike Cross, another talented musician who was also represented by Steadham. In the end, Cross landed a guest spot on the Smothers Brothers show but Gamble did not.

"One of the reasons is that Gamble could go a long ways on a story before you laughed out loud," Stafford said. "He was very careful about setting up his stories, so he might talk for a while before you got a real laugh."

Tommy Smothers didn't have the patience for that pace, Stafford said. "With Tommy you needed to really score in the first minute or two," he said. "You had to hit them hard and quick." Stafford, who professed great appreciation for Gamble's talent and storytelling technique, had the awkward task of breaking the news of the failed audition to his good friend, who seemed to take it all in stride.

Much like his fabled stories, Gamble's songs were artfully crafted. But they also had limited commercial appeal on traditional radio stations featuring the top-forty hits of the day. There were few if any radio stations whose formats included spots for such Southern Gothic laments as Gamble's "Blood Mountain" or "The Girl From Stoney Lonesome."

Where Gamble and Steadham did find an attentive market was in the rapidly growing venue of acoustic listening rooms popular in the early 1970s such as the Earl of Old Town in Chicago, the Raven Gallery in Detroit, and the Birchmere in Alexandria, Virginia. Gamble's apprenticeship at the Flick and the Tradewinds Tropical Lounge was paying dividends. Not only was his act a hit at these more established clubs, but he was revered. It was here he would forge friendships with artists headed for the national scene like Chicago's John Prine and Steve Goodman, who was best known for writing "The City of New Orleans."

While traditional radio and television never fit Gamble's style, he did find a welcoming audience on National Public Radio and several public television affiliates.

NPR used Gamble's intricate finger-picking guitar interludes for intros and station breaks. The guitar pieces were recorded at the local NPR affiliate in Gainesville and shared with the national network. He became a frequent guest commentator on NPR's *All Things Considered*, where he was invited to share his stories and songs for special programming moments.

"They would welcome his level of artistry and would invest a few extra minutes of airtime for the sake of quality programming," said Steadham.

As Gamble's agent, Steadham developed a keen sense of his client's likes and dislikes. "He knew I wouldn't deliberately put him in an uncomfortable position, not to say there weren't a handful of those," said Steadham. "If I ever booked a date he found uncomfortable he would find a polite way to let me know he'd rather not do one like that again."

One such event was a celebration in Miami for a new CEO taking the helm at *Playboy*. "They were throwing a soiree somewhere in South Beach, but it was way too artsy for Gamble's taste," recalled Steadham. "During our debriefing, he mentioned the waitstaff was running around serving hors d'oeuvres and drinks wearing codpieces. That wasn't Gamble's cup of tea."

There is widespread acknowledgement and respect among Gamble's family and friends that Steadham used his best efforts in representing his client and succeeded in his mission of securing the best payday possible while staying true to the performer's values and standards.

Meanwhile, Steadham was a firsthand witness to Gamble's talent, charisma, and compassion. They often debriefed the day after a show or after the conclusion of a tour. On one such occasion Gamble had just come off the road and was eager to return home when he was approached by a stranger in a restaurant parking lot where he and Steadham had been meeting.

"I had seen this man staring at Gamble two or three tables away," Steadham recalled. "Gamble was bone tired and desperate to get home for a number of reasons." He was physically exhausted and wanted to get back to his family. As Steadham stayed behind to pay the bill, the stranger approached Gamble in the parking lot and the two engaged in a brief conversation. Gamble, who was already in his car about to head home, followed the man out of the restaurant parking lot.

Concerned about this mysterious occurrence, Steadham phoned Gamble's home a couple of hours later only to learn he hadn't made it back. Several follow-up calls produced the same result. Once he did return home, Gamble phoned Steadham to tell him he had learned the stranger's wife was dying of cancer and was a Gamble Rogers fan. He explained to Steadham in a gracious and diplomatic way that he followed the stranger home, where he performed a private concert for the man and his dying wife.

"He didn't want or need to hear from me about how special that was," Steadham recalled. Rather, he brushed it aside, saying only that it "was really very precious."

A few years later Steadham retold the story at the St. Augustine memorial service following Gamble's untimely death. There was a gasp in the audience. It was from the deceased woman's daughter who had come to the memorial to pay her respects.

16

THERE WAS NO QUESTION that Gamble admired women and that they played a significant role in his life. From his high school romance with Joan Abendroth to his close friendship with and eventual marriage to Maggie to his fiery affair with Liz Corrigan, Gamble was in some stage of a relationship for most of his life.

His most enduring and permanent partnership was with a free-spirited, cultured woman who, like so many others, first saw Gamble perform at the Tradewinds Tropical Lounge in St. Augustine.

Nancy Lee was born in Texas in 1943 and spent much of her childhood traveling and living in Europe with her father. She spent time at a boarding school in Geneva, Switzerland, where she learned to speak French. Following high school, Nancy married and had two daughters, Stephanie and Stacy. They lived in Atlanta for a time but in 1969 moved to Jacksonville, where as a single mother by then, she started a Montessori school that her daughters attended. An avid camper, Nancy was more at home with nature, turning away from the materialistic world when possible. Much like Gamble's parents did a generation earlier, Nancy raised her children without a television set. In addition to her educational interests, she spent time working construction and tending bar.

For Gamble, a handsome, charismatic guitar picker and storyteller, meeting women was never a problem. "That's how it all started with Nancy," remembered Bob Patterson. "She presented herself as a Jacksonville debutante, but it turned out that she was really a hippie goddess woman."

"In a lot of ways she seemed Janis Joplin–like," said attorney Sid Ansbacher, a family friend.

Some accounts have Nancy meeting Gamble at the Tradewinds in the early 1970s. "Pretty much everything happened at the Tradewinds," Patterson said. "Man, if those walls could talk." Other accounts have her introducing herself to Gamble at a bluegrass concert at Pacetti's Fish Camp near Green Cove Springs, Florida. Whatever the circumstances of their meeting, there was a mutual attraction and adoration.

"She always said it was his voice that woke her up," said Nancy's granddaughter Neely Ann Miller.

"Nancy was beautiful," said Patterson. "She had a southern matriarchal aura about her. She could have stood out as a character in one of his stories."

Hookie Hamilton, a well-known St. Augustine photographer, was Gamble's neighbor when he was living in an upstairs apartment on Menendez Avenue where the popular O. C. White's Restaurant now stands. Hamilton met Gamble, at the Tradewinds, of course, when he was still with Liz Corrigan. Nancy was working construction in St. Augustine. After Gamble broke up with Liz he started seeing Nancy. Liz wanted to know more about Gamble's new romantic interest.

"I told her I didn't know her that well, but that it was a lost cause," Hamilton recalled. "It was very obvious Gamble was really in love with her and she was just head over heels with him."

Once they got together, Gamble and Nancy were constant companions. She accompanied him to many of his shows, sometimes outside of Florida and often leaving her two daughters behind to stay with friends. She was there for the important moments in his career from that point on, among them his handshake agreement with Charles Steadham to be his manager.

When Gamble wasn't performing, he and Nancy would be out camping or kayaking in matching kayaks. They traveled around St. Augustine on a couple of old-style bicycles that were easily distinguishable.

"Gamble had this ancient bike that had a sheepskin cover on the seat that looked as old as Scotland," said Ansbacher. "And, by God it was well maintained."

According to those who knew her, Nancy proved to be a good balance against an adoring public and loyal following who were used to going along with whatever Gamble had to say. "Nancy wouldn't pull any punches," said Patterson. "She'd speak the truth to him and was not afraid to be true to her own ideals. He had a lot of admiration for her."

In a remarkably candid and personal letter to Nancy dated June 8, 1977, Gamble revealed much about his life on the road, his innermost thoughts, his personal struggles, and his state of mind while in Detroit on tour.

Dear Nancy,

I'm back in a room now after having dined sumptuously on a western omelet and a plate of sliced tomatoes. I've really got a routine going here; breakfast, a forty minute walk, practice, write, supper, nap, work. Work is going beautifully, with me playing consistently at the top of my form, relaxed and enjoying every minute of it. Audiences are great—the best ever here, and growing in size this second week. (Two network affiliate T.V. shows don't hurt).

I've got to analyze why I felt so poorly for the two weeks in Gainesville, and feel so very well in this circumstance—the schedules are pretty nearly identical. Now that I think of it, I was subjected to a heavier workload and pressure from external sources in Gainesville. While there is pressure here, it is self-regulated, i.e, the discipline of writing. I have also held the line sharply here, with a result that nearly all my time is my own. Except for the T.V. and dinner Monday night with Stewart and Shirley, I've had no interaction other than what centers around the club. Anyhow, medication is the furthest thing from my mind now. I seem to have gained a little weight, but realize this probably helps me feel good, and probably won't bother with weight reduction unless chronic indigestion arises. Even now, I only weigh about 155–158.

I've begun to muse how for years, I was too impatient to submit to any external force that thwarted my sense of purpose in any way. By being so intransigent, willful, I have forever warred with inflexible forces. e.g., bus schedules, travel delays, etc., just like a child who frets when a rain storm (perfectly natural in itself) breaks up a playground session. Since we never can control externals in any way, I confess this has left me irritable at times, even needlessly chafing at the suspicion that things were bound to go against my will. You can imagine how projections of this sort have often kept me from simply sitting down to do whatever I should be doing in a relaxed, effective way. What I'm saying is that I don't feel so much at war with "things" now. The result is, I think, stronger self-belief and more effective concentration in areas where I am seemingly equipped to make the most satisfying contribution—writing, music, audience (human) communication. I realize I am happier now than ever before, and probably more effective as a human being. You've made no small contribution to the emergence of this state in me through your various advocacies and example.

I love you very much.

Gamble

Whatever differences they may have had politically or otherwise, Nancy being the more liberal one, theirs was a true love story. They shared personal journals. She charted his astrology sign. Nancy was Gamble's biggest advocate and recognized as much as anyone his ability to inspire others.

The two settled in a home in St. Augustine overlooking the Salt Run inlet in 1976. They had been housesitting for a friend when they decided to buy the residence at 27 Magnolia Drive, not far from St. Augustine's Lighthouse Park. They lived together for more than a decade before officially tying the knot at a private ceremony in the home's backyard.

"I don't think another marriage seemed like a good idea to Gamble," said Patterson. "I think for him, marriage was more of a spiritual decision between two people that didn't need all of the formalities. Somewhere along the way he got talked into it. Maybe it was because of taxes or something."

Nancy and Gamble exchanged very personal vows in front of a small group of mostly family.

Nancy: "May it be my place to bring sunshine and happiness to every day of your life and to honor your name as I stand at your side and we travel the rest of this path."

Gamble: "This also I promise, to be the husband to your heart, mind, and spirit alike and be faithful to you in body, so long as we are given to one another by provident nature, may that be forever."

Gamble's relationship and eventual marriage to Nancy didn't come without its share of complications. With two stepdaughters now added to the family fold, there was a natural rivalry for Gamble's attention, made all the more difficult by his demanding performance schedule.

"There was a lot of family stuff going on that he was called upon to handle or manage on some level," recalled Patterson. "It is a tribute to Gamble that he could stay so focused on his career and keep it moving forward in the face of things he had to deal with at home."

Lyn Rogers Lacey, Gamble's daughter from his first marriage to Maggie and his only biological progeny, said her father seemed to always find both the time and the patience for the support she needed. "He had that gift, that when he was with you, you were the most important person in the world. When he was with you, he was all there." Lyn and the other children sensed his care and concern for them even when he was away on the road, which was more often than not.

"He was a magnificent father and role model who loved all of his children unconditionally," said Stephanie Frost, one of Gamble's two stepdaughters through his marriage to Nancy.

Despite his lengthy absences, Gamble was the quintessential father figure for two separate families with one natural daughter and four stepchildren, all of whom he considered his own.

"If I was ever going through anything in life, he was always available to talk about it," Lyn recalled. "I probably didn't appreciate that until I got older because I really didn't understand the gravity of his schedule and all that he had to maneuver to be available to me."

Lyn said she was always provided a copy of her father's schedule so she knew exactly where he was performing. She remembered Gamble telling her that if she needed him and he was on stage, he'd shorten his show. "That's how he was with all of us," Lyn said, referring to her stepbrother and stepsisters. Steadham, as Gamble's manager responsible for booking his performances, said the folksinger went to great lengths to ensure his availability to his children.

From the time she was a toddler, Lyn knew the routine of the road. Gamble would get in his car on a Wednesday or Thursday, drive to his shows and be gone for the long weekend. In between there would be the simple pleasures of running routine errands together, stopping at a Dairy Queen or taking long rides or walks where she observed her father's love of nature and curiosity about the human spirit. Although she came to eventually understand her father's stature on the national folk scene, to Lyn he was "just my dad."

There were, of course, special moments. As a young adult, Lyn was teaching in Nashville when she received a call from her father. He had been asked to perform a private show for friends and family at a summer gathering at the glamorous Piedmont Driving Club in the Buckhead area of Atlanta. He wanted her to be his opening act. The two had never talked about her having a career in music even though as a child she and her stepbrother, Chuck, sometimes got called up on stage to sing harmonies with Gamble on "Two Little Boys," "The Dutchman," or Dolly Parton's "Coat of Many Colors." But this was different. Lyn had never officially opened for her father.

Although it was primarily a family performance, Gamble took it all very seriously, even having Steadham draw up a Blade Agency performance contract for Lyn.

For the show, Lyn spent months painstakingly working up an arrangement of "Georgia on My Mind." The day before the show, Gamble and Lyn walked over to the hall for a sound check. The magnificent venue with its breathtaking views of the rolling hills of Atlanta was quite a contrast to some of the places Lyn had seen her father perform. Unlike the Tradewinds, there were no salt breezes coming through the door and no blenders grinding in the background during the performance, as was often the case at some of Gamble's other haunts.

After rehearsing the songs they planned to sing together, Gamble planted a chair on the parquet floor in the middle of the empty hall and asked Lyn to perform her set for him. When she concluded, he asked if there was anything else. Lyn nervously told him about her arrangement of "Georgia on My Mind" that she had been practicing for months. He could sense her fear.

"Well, what you have to remember about playing in front of family is that if you mess up, they'll never let you forget about it," Gamble told her. "But, on the other hand they are family and they're always going to love you."

That was all Lyn needed to hear. "He had this way of looking at both sides of the coin with a little bit of philosophical humor thrown in," she said, "and these homespun truths that he was always able to pull up and it just diffused the fear."

Another moment for Lyn was a trip to New York City to see her father perform at Carnegie Hall. Gamble had been asked to emcee a folk music night at the legendary New York venue. Sharing the bill was the revered Doc Watson. The two had become good friends and performed together on several occasions. It was the fulfillment of a lifelong dream, Lyn said.

"If I could play anywhere, I'd love to play Carnegie Hall," Gamble once told Lyn.

"Is that because you think that if you play there it will mean you will have arrived?" Lyn asked.

"No, it's just that the acoustics are really good in that hall," was his humble response.

Together, father and daughter explored New York City. He took her to the Village, where Gamble and Maggie had stayed and performed in the early 1960s. He and Lyn toured St. Patrick's Cathedral, where, armed with Macy's shopping bags, they found themselves standing inadvertently in the middle of a wedding procession.

While Gamble performed his sound check, Lyn, accompanied by one of Gamble's aunts, retreated to the Russian Tea Room near the theater. A short while later, Gamble walked in. She had never seen her father dressed in a tuxedo, although she did help him shop for this particular one a month prior to the show. As he swaggered over to her table, Lyn could feel the excitement of the moment. "I just swooned," she said. "It was a magical evening. He performed so beautifully."

On the other end of the experience spectrum was a trip Lyn took with Gamble for a performance at the Peanut Gallery, a Tampa venue that featured baskets of peanuts on the tables and a floor littered with shells. It was often his practice to take long walks, when possible, before a show to keep his back limber. He and Lyn took off for a quiet walk on a nearby beach when they heard what sounded like a pulsating drum coming out of nowhere. As they continued their walk they happened upon a man sitting alone in the dunes with a motorcycle helmet on, playing a full drum set.

Gamble's quick-witted reaction was something to the effect of "Well there's someone who marches to the beat of his own drum."

In many ways, Gamble, too, marched to his own beat. Lyn and Gamble's stepchildren were privy to little things the public may not have known—his love of Ella Fitzgerald, his particular affection for the movie *Annie*, and his predilection for good barbecue and Dairy Queen. And while he had no particular use for television, he eventually owned one so he could keep track of the basketball playoffs, Lyn said.

His stepdaughter Lolly said, "I was a really lucky kid to grow up around all of this." Even in her adolescent years after Gamble and her mother divorced, Lolly took her high school and college friends to Gamble's shows and hung out with his picking pals like Crider and Patterson. "It was so much fun," she said.

When Gamble became involved with Nancy, her two daughters, Stephanie and Stacy, became an integral part of his life. Nancy's girls had their own treasured memories of a doting father and grandfather. Stephanie recalled how on special holidays like Christmas and Easter, Gamble would personally go to St. Augustine's Cassie's Carousel dress shop and pick out dresses for the girls. "He would take his big binder checkbook under his arm and ride his bike down there and come back with these frilly dresses," Stephanie said. "He would pick them out himself. He wouldn't send our mother. It was his thing."

"When he would come home from a trip, his first priority would be to get us all together as a family," she said. Despite having just spent days on the road, Gamble piled the family into his car for a night out at a favorite restaurant, even if it was miles away.

At least outwardly, he never seemed overwhelmed by his personal responsibilities in the midst of building his professional career. "He was being truthful to his calling, and those of us in his life didn't ever resent it," Lyn said. "He was fiercely dedicated and true to what he was good at and what he was predisposed to do with his life. He didn't try to be all things to all people, but in a sense, that's what he ended up doing. That's one of the mysteries about him."

17

The stories I tell are all true except the few that are obviously whimsy.

—GAMBLE ROGERS

LIKE SO MUCH ELSE IN HIS LIFE, Gamble Rogers's storytelling was an evolutionary process.

A myriad of factors were at play. There was his self-proclaimed "misspent youth" when he was flat on his back reading everything from the classics to the dictionary while protecting his back from a potentially crippling spinal fusion. There were his childhood summers in the Nacoochee Valley, where the authenticity of the agrarian culture left a lasting impression. There was the literary Southern Gothic influence of William Faulkner, and there was Gamble's own keen intellect, sense of humor, and innate curiosity. He used the characters and locales he'd encountered along the way to explain the human condition as he saw it. As complex and intricately woven as his stories were, with his mastery of the English language and his voluminous vocabulary, Gamble was often just stating the obvious. "Horse sense," he called it.

In his early performances, Gamble professed to have been raised in the "Coochee Valley" of Georgia. The characters and tales he spun were set in the backdrop of those Georgia foothills. But Florida was his real home, and over time he changed the theme and setting to his native state.

"They were the very same characters and the same stories he had been telling that were originally based in Georgia," said Jim Carrick.

He remembered Gamble saying, "I'm from Florida. I summered in Georgia and a lot of these stories came out of there, but I'm going to turn this around to be Florida."

The result was the creation of the apocryphal Oklawaha County, a rural North Florida setting where "everybody in town knows what everybody else is doing, but we still read the newspaper to see who got caught at it."

Snipes Ford served as the mythical county seat and center of literacy and was "notable for its outsized number of rural alchemists," Gamble proclaimed. "It's not what you are thinking. We have an inordinate number of folks who spend the bulk of their waking hours puzzling out novel ways to bleach their used coffee grounds so they can sell them to the tourists on the interstate for grits . . . which goes a long way to explaining why so many northerners don't care a hoot for southern cooking."

In addition to the rural alchemists, the county was populated with production fishermen, all of whom had the last name Jones, "a genus of aquatic entrepreneurs characterized by incredible resourcefulness, adventuresome approach, breathtaking balance, and dynamite."

And then there were the metaphysicians, the philosophers led by Agamemnon Jones. They assembled at the loading ramp of Erindale's Purina Store to preach the aphorisms of the day.

Experience is what you get when you didn't get what you really want.
An expert is an ordinary man away from home.
Let them that don't want none have memories of never getting any.
It is always easier to get forgiveness than it is to get permission.
Never talk metric to decent folk.

In the truest folk tradition, many of these were adaptions of humorous quotations that had been around for decades. It was how Gamble applied them in his stories that gave them new meaning and context.

Often these aphorisms would be reserved for the punch line to deliver the message or drive home the point about one of life's ironies. The messenger was usually one of Oklawaha's own such as Agamemnon Jones or one of the many other sordid characters who populated the fictional county. Among them were

The Reverend Jeremiah Proudfoot of the Bean Creek Baptist Church, whose sermon was once interrupted by a 2,400-pound Brahma bull that came crashing through the wall of the sanctuary after having been shot with a BB gun by young Shelby III.

Shelby III, the youngest of eleven cousins, whose name told you three things: "He was a Republican, an Episcopalian, and an overachiever."

Narcissa Nonesuch, a community organizer.

Forklift Mary, a lover of literature and member of the William Faulkner Literary Society.

Penrod, a retired kamikaze pilot for the Confederate Cropduster's Association and a commode-hugging drunk.

Oklawaha County's most notable resident was Still Bill, a sorry figure of a man who moved so slowly you had to line him up against a fencepost to see if he was in fact really moving. Bill could never seem to win for losing, despite his best intentions. On one occasion his noble efforts at home repair backfired when his wife, War Bunny, a righteous woman, found herself haplessly stuck to the newly re-enameled toilet seat for seven and a half excruciating hours. Gamble implored his audience to visualize along with him Still Bill attempting to free his wife from "the accommodation."

Bill was frequently seen alongside his three-legged Chihuahua, a symbol of canine obedience. "Dear people, it takes a compassionate man to covet a three-legged-dog," Gamble declared. "And it takes a sorry son of a gun to name that dog Flat Tire."

Gamble used an encounter with Still Bill, who was trying to trade Flat Tire for .22 caliber rifle, to make his own distinction between dogs and "dawgs."

D-A-W-G. That's real McCoy I'm talking about. Lovable, loyal, and lop-eared. Bring you brandy when you are lost in a snowdrift, follow you over the blazing desert sands 'til he bloodies and blisters his faithful little feet, lay his grizzled snoot up on your knee and look up at you with those big limpid brown eyes and say, "I love you. I'm a dawg."

Then there's dogs, D-O-G-S, yip yaps, weigh about a pound and a half a piece, bejeweled, beribboned, pomaded, powdered, painted toenails, rhinestone collars, designed by God and nature to be trawled in the wake of a slow-moving boat in search of large trash fish such as a hammerhead shark. Yip yaps, canine closet queens.

Gamble clearly preferred dawgs and was the proud owner of a hound named Seeger (in honor of Peter Seeger) as his canine companion. The two walked the neighborhood near the lighthouse in St. Augustine whenever Gamble was in town. It was a familiar sight.

"The way Gamble would walk down the street always reminded me of a pair of pliers," said Bob Patterson. Seeger, the hound, often sat in on the nightly jam sessions at Gamble's house. The two would look back and forth at each other as if they were communicating in their own silent language. Gamble waited for Seeger to start licking himself and said, "I sure wish I could do that."

Gamble's Oklawaha County was not just known for its raffish residents. There were the familiar landmarks as well.

Erindale's Purina Store and loading ramp, where the rural philosophers gathered to teach the difference between judgment and experience.

Bean Creek Baptist Church, complete with its own SWAT team.

Snipes Ford Live Bait Livery and Marine Laundry, owned by Neon Leon, who doubled as the county's bail bondsman.

The Terminal Tavern, a "temple of culture" on Redbug Road between Snipes Ford and Bean Creek.

Most of the people and places were based on Gamble's own childhood experiences in Winter Park or his summers in Nacoochee Valley. Yet he transformed them into lively homespun tales that connected with his audience in a distinctively folksy manner in spite of his use of multisyllable "twenty dollar" words.

"Some people may have used these words in such a way that would put others off," said Lyn. "His use of these words endeared people to him and pulled them in even more."

Gamble's storytelling style drew inevitable comparisons to Garrison Keillor and his *Prairie Home Companion* radio show, which attained national acclaim on public radio. While they were considered contemporaries, Gamble's appearances on NPR predated Keillor's radio show. Moreover, the residents of Keillor's fictitious Lake Wobegon, Minnesota, could not have been more different than the southern "pilgrims" who populated Oklawaha County. In Keillor's Lake Wobegon, "The women are strong, the men are handsome, and the children above average." In contrast, Bean Creek in Oklawaha County is best described as a primitive place where sorriness was a virtue. From his "Bean Creek Alphabet" comes this depiction:

> They're so primitive in Bean Creek, the Baptist Church has a SWAT team. They're so primitive in Bean Creek, they don't even have an alphabet. If they want to write something down, they just draw a bunch of pictures. And I submit to you that a symbolic alphabet is the very cornerstone of communication. In Bean Creek, the word for "house" is a square, the perfect symbol of habitation, four walls. Their word for "woman" is a circle—alpha, omega, the earth, the earth mother. Their word for "man" is a straight line. Thus, when they express a concept in Bean Creek such as "home," they draw a square containing a circle and a straight line. Their word for "trouble" is a square with a straight line and two circles.

In a 1987 interview for the *Orlando Sentinel's Florida Magazine*, Gamble said he found the comparisons to Keillor "flattering," although he was quick to point out their differences and to give due credit to the storytellers who preceded them.

"My stories, for instance, are either set to music or have music interspersed with them while his is strictly a spoken narrative," he told the reporter. "But neither of us originated the device of creating an apocryphal community. Edgar Lee Masters, with Spoon River, William Faulkner and Mark Twain are but a few who preceded us in that regard."

Gamble delivered his moralizing discourses with a preacher-like cadence that alternated between a tent revival sermon and a fireside chat. His timing and delivery were carefully crafted. He would frequently begin a story by talking over an intricate fingerpicking backdrop only to suddenly stop, swing the guitar behind his back, and resume the story without so much as missing a beat. His lengthy shows were rapidly paced.

"His real art was that once he hit the stage there was no time for the audience to really think whether they liked it or not," said Jim Carrick. "He never gave you chance. He only gave the audience two or three opportunities to applaud at a show."

As a result, the same audiences returned to hear something they may have missed the first time around. Gamble obliged. While he was constantly tweaking his act, he knew the stories that worked, and he did his best to perfect them rather than tossing them away in favor of fresher material at each performance.

"He got to a point where he stuck with the winners," said Carrick.

Folksinger James Lee Stanley said that was the lesson he learned from Gamble early in his career. Stanley met Gamble at Charlotte's Web in Rockford, Illinois.

"He was a remarkable musician, very nurturing and the embodiment of a southern gentleman," Stanley said. Like other artists at the time, Stanley was using monologues to accompany his songs, especially during interludes when he would tune his guitar.

"I used to feel compelled to change the stories or come up with new ones every night," Stanley said. "I learned from Gamble that stories were an art form, not to be thrown away. People will want to hear the same stories night after night just as they like to hear the same songs."

Gamble's audiences were as familiar with his stories as they might be with the lyrics of their favorite tunes. And while Gamble enjoyed getting laughs by poking fun at Still Bill, Downwind Dave, and other residents of Oklawaha County, he never portrayed himself to be above them. In fact, he considered himself to be among them and savored the glorious honor of having been proclaimed "the Troubadour Emeritus of Oklawaha County, a place where second chances abound."

18

~~~~~~~~~~~~~~~~~~

The Lord gives me grace, and the devil gives me style.

—Gamble Rogers

While the characters and tales of Oklawaha County were establishing Gamble as a storyteller and folklorist, there was no minimizing his talent as a singer-songwriter. His musical themes ran the gamut from the light-hearted to the macabre. He waxed poetically about love and death, morality and murder, war and human suffering. His lyrics could make people laugh or cry. Like his stories, his songs commanded undivided attention.

"Every song was literature," said Gamble's longtime agent and manager, Charles Steadham. "His songs were self-described Southern Gothic art songs. They were very heavy, very artfully written, very thick. These were not 'Let's get drunk and drive the pickup truck down to the lake' country songs. There was all this brilliance, all of this profound understanding and perception of human drama."

Murder was a familiar theme. "Doris" was one of Gamble's most stirring compositions. Before beginning the song he would offer this haunting prologue:

Doris moved among the towering enchantments of old St. Augustine, her hair in a long pigtail, wearing clothing she made of Irish linen. Always, it seemed, in the company of someone who instinctively sought her out to share the treasure of their heart. She would listen ardently to what they'd said, and they would go away more graceful for having been listened to by this creature who spurned the pipe, who spurned the bottle, who loved the salt air and the sunlight, and who hated only cruelty. She, who died at the hands of one of those with whom she walked, who now lies buried in St. Augustine and is remembered by poems and elegies and eulogies, by painting and statuary. For the Ancient City is a place of artists and writers as well as fools and fisherman.

The introduction was so recognizable that Gamble fans could recite it verbatim.

The more serious side also permeates songs like "Blood Mountain," "Good Causes" (coauthored with Forest Carpenter), "Alabaster Sally," and "Color Becoming Grace" a dark southern tale about a boy with a shadow eye and club foot. "This could have easily been a Flannery O'Conner story," Charlie Robertson told *Folio Weekly* in a 1993 interview.

There were the lighter tunes as well, replete with Gamble's humorous take on familiar subjects like women and whiskey. "Black Label Blues," "Long Legged Women," "Mama Blue," and "Home Grown Lucifer (Habersham County Mephistopheles)" were Gamble originals that danced with a dose of satire and sweetness.

Given his guitar-picking prowess, it was inevitable that Gamble's musical catalogue would include several elaborate fingerpicking instrumentals. "Deep Gap Salute" was among his most famous. The improvisational, spirited melody is a tribute to Gamble's friend and guitar hero Doc Watson, who hailed from Deep Gap, North Carolina. Gamble revered Watson, who was considered to be among the most talented and influential flat-top guitar players ever.

Blind since early childhood, Watson was a national treasure and shared a lot in common with Gamble. Both were disciples of the Merle Travis style of fingerpicking, which uses the thumb and finger to alternately pick the bass and treble strings. The sound is unmistakable, particularly when performed by the likes of Doc Watson or Gamble Rogers. The two also shared a similar dignity, grace, and humility in the way they carried themselves. "Deep Gap Salute" or some derivative was a Gamble standard at his performances. He always made it a point to give credit to his musical influences, particularly Doc Watson, Merle Travis, and Chet Atkins.

It was Gamble's interpretations or covers of other works that often drew the most critical acclaim. His rendition of John Stewart's "July You're a Woman" was a crowd favorite. While he stayed true to the Stewart original, the song blended naturally with Gamble's smooth voice and guitar-picking style.

Always a proud southerner, Gamble Rogers included songs in his extensive repertoire that were set in the Civil War era. A favorite was Don Oja Dunaway's "Kennesaw Line." The song defiantly declares, "And I pity the poor Yankee bastards who died so far from home."

Some of his best covers were songs he learned as a child from his father, the architect.

"Here's one of those songs my daddy used to sing to make my mama's eyes change color" is how Gamble introduced his version of the poignant "Two Little Boys," a sentimental Civil War tearjerker composed by Theodore Morse, with lyrics by Edward Madden.

No cover is more associated with Gamble Rogers than Michael Peter Smith's "The Dutchman." Smith had written "The Dutchman" in the late 1960s, and it quickly became a popular cover song for folk musicians. Set in Amsterdam, "The Dutchman" is a sad but tender tale of unconditional love between the unnamed aging Dutchman and Margaret, who has cared for him, knows his secrets, and sees "her unborn children in his eyes."

"In the real world," Gamble would say before playing the song, "there's just two kinds of love. There's love and there's luuuuv. Here's a luuuv song."

Smith said he was aware that Gamble was among those performing "The Dutchman" and was flattered. "It was a big deal to me that anyone was doing one of my songs at all," said Smith. "He was very complimentary to me about the song and had an elaborate way of praising a given lyric or moment. It was thrilling to me that this very bright man was calling me out as a good songwriter."

Smith, meanwhile, had his own appreciation of Gamble's writing talent. "The songs that he wrote were so esoteric, so rococo," said Smith. "His songs were highly poetic, like a southern Edgar Allan Poe." What struck Smith was that when Gamble performed "The Dutchman" alongside his own stories and tunes, it seemed like it belonged.

"He translated it for people," said Smith. "He learned a song that would not be the first thing you would necessarily expect from him. Yet he found a way of playing it where it fit into the sensibility of the people he was playing for."

It was Gamble's connectivity with the audience that set him apart. "Let's say Gamble was playing one of the typical places Gamble played," Smith explained. "He could play my song, and if I got up after him and played the same song they would love it by him but be puzzled about it by me. They wouldn't even pay attention."

Smith had that exact experience at the Tradewinds Tropical Lounge in St. Augustine. At Gamble's urging, Smith played the Tradewinds. "He told me they would love me at the Tradewinds," Smith said. "Well, I played the Tradewinds, and it was a raucous, yelling bar where nobody shut up for a minute. That was my experience at the Tradewinds."

Smith witnessed what defined Gamble and his relationship to his audience and his art. "What I saw was that Gamble managed to figure out a way to make people sit up and pay attention that had nothing to do with the guitar or the words he was singing," Smith said. "It was due, in part, because he was willing to talk to people in that patented Gamble way. But primarily it was because he made the music intelligible for people who wouldn't get what I was doing."

It wasn't Gamble's or Michael Peter Smith's version of "The Dutchman" that was the most commercially successful. That honor belonged to their mutual friend and contemporary Steve Goodman. The Chicago-based singer-songwriter began performing his version of "The Dutchman" around the same time as Gamble. "I thought Gamble's version was the more accurate one," said Smith. The diminutive Goodman had great stage presence. He and Gamble formed a close personal relationship before Goodman's battle with leukemia took his life in 1984 at the age of thirty-six.

Gamble's version of "The Dutchman" typically evoked an emotional response from his audience as they quietly sang along at the chorus:

Let us go to the banks of the ocean,
Where the walls rise above the Zeider Zee.
Long ago I used to be a young man
And dear Margaret remembers that for me.

For the song's composer, Gamble's version had an enduring impact.

"What he did with 'The Dutchman' was to sort of ensure me some kind of employment in Florida for the rest of my life," said Smith with a chuckle.

At his live performances, Gamble weaved his unique brand of storytelling, instrumental interludes, original compositions, and popular song covers into a rapid-fire, free-flowing show that eventually became the foundation of his act.

"Oklawaha County laissez-faire" is what Gamble called it: "Take it easy, boy, but take it greasy. Let the rough end ride and the slick end slide. That's Oklawaha County laissez-faire."

Who else but Gamble could juxtapose a story about the removal of port-a-lets ("The Honeydipper") and follow it with the poignancy of a tender love ballad? Yet he somehow made it work and took his audiences along with him.

To be fully appreciated, his long-form art needed to be experienced in its entirety. A brief radio snippet or a television guest spot couldn't do it justice. It was in the popular listening rooms of places named Applejacks, the Last Resort, and the Exit Inn that audiences could gather and experience firsthand Oklawaha County laissez-faire.

19

~~~~~~~~~~~~~~~~~~~~~

I ain't nothing but a whiskey salesman.

—Gamble Rogers

On October 10, 1975, the popular folksinger Harry Chapin was preparing for a sold-out show at Jacksonville's Civic Auditorium. Just about a mile south, across the St. Johns River, Mike Schneider and his business partners were hatching a plan for the opening night of music at the recently renovated venue they named Applejacks, in the San Marco neighborhood.

For Applejacks' first night of entertainment, they had booked a former Jacksonville University basketball player turned musician, Mike Denney. "He did a lot of Harry Chapin music," recalled Schneider. "We got the idea we could book him to coincide with the end of the Harry Chapin concert downtown."

Schneider and his wife, Terry, along with another Applejacks employee headed to the concert's downtown parking lot armed with a thousand or so handbills, which they placed on car windshields. "If you love Harry Chapin, you'll love Mike Denney" was the handbill's message, to encourage concertgoers to hop over to Applejacks on their way home from the Chapin concert. The ploy worked. Applejacks was jammed. It was the beginning of a successful run for the intimate San Marco bar that tapped into a relatively new but popular club format—a listening room where the emphasis was on the performer.

Such clubs were popping up everywhere. The Night Flight in Savannah and Harrigan's in Winter Park were among those familiar to Schneider.

"We took the concept of the listening room literally," Schneider recalled. "We were anal about trying to create or preserve the performance environment." On the night of a ticketed performance, Applejacks had tabletop reminders to the patrons requesting that they keep their conversations to a minimum during the performance. At first there was resistance.

"In the beginning, there was a learning curve, and we had to school our audience," Schneider said. "Invariably we would have to go out and tap people on the shoulder."

After a while the audiences got the message. Not all the acts required that kind of attention. But those that did were afforded the opportunity to play without the interference of a drunken heckler or an unruly crowd.

With his growing reputation and carefully crafted act, Gamble Rogers was a must-have performer at these popular venues. His manager, Charles Steadham, had mastered the listening-room landscape. "A lot of the performers we booked came through Charles Steadham," Schneider said.

Whenever Gamble appeared at Applejacks, he usually brought with him a loyal following. If people had never heard Gamble, they came because they had been encouraged by someone else. "They weren't just coming for an office party," said Schneider. "They were coming to experience Gamble Rogers."

On stage, Oklawaha County laissez-faire was in full bloom. Gamble was constantly perfecting the art of weaving his stories in and out, between, during, and after selected songs, accompanied by a finger-picking, toe-tapping acoustic backdrop. He often performed two and sometimes three shows a night, Schneider said. His physical presence on stage was something to behold. "He never seemed to have an off night when he was on stage," Schneider said.

At closing time, Schneider and Gamble sat at a table across from each other to settle up. "He was never real comfortable in that setting," Schneider recalled. Gamble's contract usually called for a guarantee and a certain percentage of the gate. If Gamble felt the crowd was a little thin, he would ask how much they had taken in at the front door. If there wasn't the usual number of customers, Gamble refused to accept the agreed-upon fee, something Schneider and his partners were always prepared to pay. "You're not going to pay me because I didn't bring them in," Gamble told Schneider on one such occasion. He said, "It just wouldn't be right." Instead, he proposed a reduced fee based on the night's crowd.

"He cared about the owners of these clubs," said Gamble's daughter Lyn. "He knew they had families and bills to pay too."

It was a business ethic Schneider had never seen from any other performer. It was quite a contrast from a story Schneider said he once heard about rhythm-and-blues artist Ike Turner. According to the story, Turner went to a club manager's office to collect his performance fee. When the manager tried to short him, Turner pulled out a long-barrel .38 caliber gun and proclaimed he would get his money one way or another.

With Steadham's aggressive bookings, Gamble covered the road map of listening rooms across North America, the Last Resort in Athens, Georgia, the Raven Gallery in Detroit, the Earl of Old Town in Chicago. He liked to return to the same venues over and over. Wherever he performed there was likely a loyal following in attendance. Fortunately, thin crowds were the exception, especially as Gamble's reputation grew on the listening-room circuit.

Veteran singer-songwriter Rod MacDonald was the opening act for Gamble on a variety of occasions. MacDonald remembered a particular gig at Tampa's Peanut Gallery, where they were booked for two shows on the same evening. For the first show, Gamble performed his regular set, pacing the stage, guitar behind his back, telling stories, and singing songs to an attentive and appreciative audience that filled the room.

The club wasn't cleared between shows, so a handful of patrons remained behind. With a smaller, more intimate audience for the second show, Gamble pulled up a stool and quietly just started playing the guitar. "I think his back had been bothering him," MacDonald recalled. "He said he was just going to sit and pick a bit this set." One by one, the remaining patrons, some of whom were guitar players themselves, gathered around the stage and witnessed a remarkable impromptu performance in which Gamble dispensed with his regular act in favor of the spontaneity of the moment. "To this day," MacDonald said, "that remains the most favorite set I ever saw Gamble play."

By the mid-1970s Gamble was attracting more national attention, helped in part by his appearances on National Public Radio and his exhaustive performance schedule. He was being featured at larger venues, often as the opening act for well known artists on tour.

Larry Mangum, a North Florida musician who was trying his hand at concert promotion, thought he had hit a jackpot when with the help of Steadham he booked the Earl Scruggs Revue with special guest Gamble Rogers at the Jacksonville Civic Auditorium on June 27, 1976. Mangum, who expected a crowd of about two thousand, invested $10,000 in the show.

Whether by coincidence or not, another area promoter, Sidney Drashin, booked the J. Geils Band and Charlie Daniels on the same night as Mangum's show at the larger Jacksonville Veteran's Memorial Coliseum. "I'm just guessing because I never met the guy, but he shut down my show," Mangum recalled.

Mangum's worst fears were realized. A sparse crowd of five hundred attended. Although the Civic Auditorium was more than three quarters empty, it didn't stop Gamble from delivering a hard-driving, fast-paced, energetic performance. "It's one of the best concerts you will ever hear Gamble do live," said Mangum, who recorded the show.

For Mangum the concert was a financial flop. He lost $7,000. "I remember the bus driving away with Earl Scruggs that night with these big chrome, beautiful hub caps, and I thought, there goes my $7,000," he said. It was the end of the promotion business for Mangum, who continued on as successful musician and songwriter.

Inspired in part by hearing Gamble say on stage, "Ain't it great to be alive and be in Florida?" Mangum wrote a popular song using the phrase as its title. He composed three tribute ballads to Gamble including the emotional "The Last Troubadour," which won first place at the 2005 Gamble Rogers Music Festival in St. Augustine.

Wherever he traveled, Gamble seemed to leave his footprint and some measure of influence on those whose paths he crossed. Before his days as a megastar, Jimmy Buffett spent considerable time with Gamble traversing the folk club circuit in the front seat of the lime green fastback Mustang. At the time, it was Gamble who was the headliner offering words of wisdom and encouragement to the up-and-coming singer. Buffett opened for Gamble in taverns like the Tradewinds in St. Augustine and the Hub Pub Club in Buoy's Creek, North Carolina.

As Buffett's star emerged, he returned the favor, asking Gamble to open for him at various venues. When Buffett launched his first Margaritaville Cafe in Key West in 1988, he invited Gamble to be the inaugural performer. Buffett dedicated his 1994 *Fruitcakes* CD to Gamble's memory; he acknowledged in the liner notes that he was the "apprentice" and Gamble was the "master."

At the Tradewinds Tropical Lounge, near the stage is a framed letter in which Buffett pays homage to his teacher and friend. It reads,

> One of the untold, but essential qualities of life as a troubadour is that you teach your code to those you feel deserve and can handle the knowledge of performing. Gamble was my teacher. Our classroom was his fastback Mustang or a barstool at the Tradewinds, or a bench in Peacock Park in Coconut Grove. . . .
>
> Gamble Rogers taught me how to move an audience with dialogue and delivery as much as with music. I attribute a lot of my ability to remain true to my vision to Gamble Rogers and what he taught me.

In his book *A Pirate Looks at Fifty*, Buffett recalled an example of the advice he received from his mentor in dealing with an overzealous fan: Have patience. "They still love you despite their bad manners."

Gamble took pride in the success of others, especially those he mentored. As for his own commercial success, or lack thereof, Gamble seemed to be at ease. While his live audiences were loyal and enthusiastic, he lacked a major recording contract that might have heightened his commercial appeal. His daughter Lyn said the offers were there if he had been so inclined. He opted instead for autonomy.

"I love the scale of what I'm doing," Gamble told her. "When you start reaching for things that are bigger than what you are or what you were meant to be, you start imitating yourself."

Gamble saw the music business "as a meat and potatoes operation," Lyn said. It didn't stop him from attracting a large and loyal following who connected with him and his brand of artistic authenticity. He became a star to the people with whom he was most comfortable, and he performed where he was most at ease. He had a particular affinity for folk festivals like those in Philadelphia and in his home state of Florida, where he became both a symbol and spokesperson for the Florida folk scene.

20

Sometimes the best stories are lies, but they may be the most pretty things you've ever heard. So, I'm leery of researching things in case I find out they are not true.

—GAMBLE ROGERS

IT WAS THE IDYLLIC SETTING of the Florida Folk Festival on the banks of the Suwannee River where Gamble Rogers would become known as the symbolic leader of the Florida folk movement and establish himself as Florida's troubadour.

The Florida Folk Festival debuted on May 8, 1953, at the Stephen Foster Memorial Park in White Springs. Against a backdrop of tall pines, ancient oaks, and beautiful magnolias, the three-day festival was a cultural exposition of square dancing, folk music, rope skipping, fiddle playing, and storytelling. The performers were an amalgamation of Native Americans, immigrants, schoolchildren, African Americans, and Florida Crackers, all displaying an array of cultural customs and heritages.

The inaugural festival was deemed a huge success and set the stage for the establishment of an annual pilgrimage to White Springs. It was at the Florida Folk Festival where visitors could learn such crafts as bonnet and apron making and attend workshops on whip cracking, hog calling, and water witching, the uncanny art of pinpointing water with a divining rod. There were Maypole dancers, whistlers, Seminole Indian storytellers, and folksingers. Under the direction of the colorful and dynamic "Cousin" Thelma Boltin, the Florida Folk Festival soon became the signature event for celebrating Florida's rich cultural history and traditions.

A little-known Gamble Rogers made his first appearance on the main stage of the Florida Folk Festival in 1963. There he performed a "homemade song that pays homage to the animals" ("The Masterbuilders") and a "song of sentiment" ("Two Little Boys"). Preceding Gamble on stage was Will McLean, who was also making his Florida Folk Festival main stage debut. For Gamble, it was the beginning of a twenty-eight-year relationship with the festival at which he ascended to the dual role of headliner and guiding spirit of the annual spring gathering on the Suwannee.

"A lot of people say White Springs isn't White Springs without the great national and Florida treasure, Gamble Rogers," is how Dennis Devine introduced Gamble at the 1987 festival.

Frank Thomas, widely recognized as the dean of Florida folk music, remembered being introduced to Gamble at the Florida Folk Festival by their mutual friend Will McLean. Thomas said he first heard about Gamble from Paul Champion. "I knew if he could play anything like Paul Champion he must be something special," Thomas said. Thomas wasn't disappointed. "When I heard him for the first time at the folk festival I thought, oh my God, I've never heard anything like that."

Thomas has performed his own unique brand of Florida songs for decades. To the folksinging community, Thomas, who performed for years with his late wife, Ann, is nothing short of a true Florida legend. "I ain't nothing extree," he likes to proclaim. "I'm just an old cracker who loves the state of Florida and writes songs about it." He lives in a modest home deep in the woods in Lake Wales off Rattlesnake Road. A favorite pastime is holding court on the front porch of his house, affectionately known as the Cracker Palace.

Thomas was part of a dedicated group of Florida folksingers who looked to Gamble as their leader and inspiration. "He was a great musician, but he was also the patriarch of this circle we call Florida music," Thomas said. "He was the high man and he took this role very seriously."

Thomas recalled a year at the Florida Folk Festival when some newly arrived immigrants from Vietnam were invited to perform a dance routine. Thomas was not too happy and questioned what Vietnamese dancers had to do with Florida. Gamble, seizing on the knowledge that Thomas had recently adopted a biracial child, responded, "Listen Frank, we are all the adopted children of the state of Florida. Would you deny your younger siblings a place at the table?" When put in that context, Thomas was speechless. "He just put it right out there in a way you can understand."

Gamble set forth a similar case in defending the performance of the noted gospel and blues singer Diamond Teeth Mary, whose appearance at the Florida Folk Festival drew objections from some of the festival's longtime purists who couldn't understand what a gospel and blues singer was doing at a folk festival.

Like he did during his days at the Tradewinds, Gamble used his stature at the Florida Folk Festival to open doors for other performers. In turn, the festival afforded Gamble the opportunity to perform on stage with his closest friends as well as newcomers he was bringing on to the scene in a variety of formats and settings. In spite of his demanding performance schedule, Gamble understood the importance of his presence at the festival. There were certainly more financially rewarding gigs. But the Florida Folk Festival was at the very heart of Gamble's passion for his craft and his home state.

From the mid-1970s until his death, Gamble was among the festival's dominant figures. He was often called upon to close the show, and he emceed tributes to friends who preceded him in death like Paul Champion in 1986 and Will McLean in 1990.

In the mid-1980s Gamble hosted a popular festival event known as the Liars Workshop. It was there in 1987 that Gamble unmasked the truth about his life and his art form in a compelling and remarkably revealing presentation. In the one-hour workshop, preserved by the Florida Archives, he spoke of influences like Abraham Lincoln and William Faulkner and paid homage to a college professor, Mr. Disque, who Gamble said taught him one of the most important lessons he ever learned.

Disque was a design professor at the University of Virginia, where Gamble was studying architecture. He described Disque as having a "mane of white hair, a feisty mustache, and kind of shambled when he walked." On the first day of class, Disque administered a one-question test: "How many columns are there on the front of this building?" There were eighteen people in class, and only two answered correctly. "Five years later they were at the head of the class," Gamble said.

The lesson was that details matter. "That was some of the best advice I ever had, in or out of college," Gamble told the workshop participants. "If anybody wants to tell a story or write a novel, paint a picture or design a building, if they are aware of details then they are off to a good start. Finally, that's the way stories are built, detail after detail after detail."

Gamble also spoke of his other great influence in college, William Faulkner. He explained that early in his career Faulkner went to New Orleans to seek advice from his mentor Sherwood Anderson. A successful author in his own right, Anderson told Faulkner the best thing he could do would be to return to Oxford, Mississippi, and write about subjects from his own hometown. Years later, after Faulkner had won the Nobel Prize, he acknowledged that by returning home and writing about his native soil he found more stories than he could have written in a lifetime.

"So if anybody wants to tell stories, the best place to start is right in your own backyard," said Gamble. "Start with your own family and move out." That was Gamble's blueprint.

Since he was conducting a liars workshop, Gamble had no choice than to speak about the art of lying. "Every time my mother hears that I'm going to a folk festival and performing at a liars workshop she looks hurt and her lower lip starts to quiver," Gamble said. "That's a very dangerous sign for my mother."

He went on to explain the subtleties of lying as an art form. "A lie is not necessarily a prevarication or a mendacity," Gamble said. "It's just a peculiar slant to things. Storytellers have always understood this."

He used none other than "Honest Abe" Lincoln to make his point. According to his biographers, Lincoln had a habit of repeating the same story over and over again to any number of people he would encounter in the course of a day. The stories were often repeated in the presence of Lincoln's Springfield law partner William Herndon, who found the repetition annoying. When he confronted Lincoln as to why he found it necessary to repeat the same story over and over again, Lincoln replied that the sole purpose of such repetition was to make the story a little better each time he retold it.

"And so it is, with the retelling the storyteller can chip away with things, almost as if the story has form," Gamble said. He continued by explaining some of the liberties he took with his own stories, using his uproarious tale of Shelby III and the Brahma bull as an example.

The short summary of the performance version is that Gamble's youngest cousin, ten-year-old Shelby III, was outside testing his new Daisy Red Rider lever-action BB gun when one of his shots hit a 2,400-pound Brahma bull "squarely in the seat of his sovereignty." The dead-on shot caused the bull to fly through the air and crash through the altar wall of the Bean Creek Baptist Church at the precise moment the preacher was delivering a sermon on "the Beast of the Apocalypse." Gamble said the story was true, right down to the boy's name, the make of the BB gun, and the wounded, bellowing bull.

> The fact that the bull ran up the fence line and kicked a hole in the wall of an actual Presbyterian church is a minor detail. And I'll grant you even there was not a sermon in progress in the building when this great tumult and clanging transpired, but that is of little consequence. There could have been a sermon in progress. And if there had been a sermon in progress, how rich and wonderful would it be to have the minister fulminating on the Beast of the Apocalypse. That sort of thing is in the air. This is not lying or prevarication. This is merely fleshing out a story.

For Gamble, the real truth behind the story was that his young cousin, Shelby III, did not want to lose his new BB gun after shooting the bull. Someone had to render up an accounting of what had happened to the family's elders. "It was always my blessing to be able to tell exactly what happened without deviating one wit, but add just enough to convince the elders that while I wasn't lying, something funny had happened," Gamble said. "If they laughed, my young cousin got to keep his BB gun. That's when I learned that storytelling, besides being entertaining, has utility."

In the span of the one-hour workshop Gamble offered his version of the Golden Rule of storytelling. "The trick to satire or poking fun at people and institutions is to poke as much fun at yourself as you do at anybody else." The stories shouldn't focus on victims, Gamble explained. "But rather choose your characters for their heroic propensities and glorify that, because heroism is all around us. It is perfectly alright to have a victim if you extricate the victim later on or let the victim redeem themselves or carry the day and become a hero. That makes it all the more rich."

21

~~~~~~~~~~~~~~

IN LESS THAN A DECADE after leaving the limelight of the Serendipity Singers, Gamble Rogers had forged his identity as a highly regarded solo artist and the titular head of the Florida folk music scene. Despite a demanding road schedule that often left him exhausted and in physical discomfort, Gamble still found the time and energy to engage in a number of other projects and good causes he deemed important.

"He slept only four hours a night," remembered Jim Carrick. "As soon as he got up, everything was on a schedule. Walk, breakfast, read, and so on."

Among his most passionate personal crusades was the preservation and restoration of the scenic Ocklawaha River in Central Florida that serves as the principal tributary to the St. Johns River. Considered one of the state's great natural resources, the Ocklawaha has suffered significant ecological damage from pollution, fertilizer runoff, and dredging. The river's location has made it a political lightning rod for the battle between business interests and conservationists. It was at the center of the controversy over the proposed Cross Florida Barge Canal in the 1960s and 1970s. The river, which is cut off by the Rodman Dam, is still the subject of an ongoing tussle pitting ecology and science against pork-barrel politics.

"Gamble hated what was being done to the Ocklawaha," said Bob Patterson, who carries his own passion for restoring and protecting the river. Patterson remains convinced that Gamble's fictionalized Oklawaha County was so named to keep the river forever memorialized. (Gamble's Oklawaha County does not contain the letter "c" as in the spelling of the river.)

One of Gamble's favorite organizations was the Nature Conservancy. Patterson recalled, "He liked how they planned to buy land piece by piece and then stitch them together like a quilt as it became possible. He wanted any money donated to him to go to them."

While not political by nature, Gamble did use his influence and stature to lobby for environmental causes and to keep commercial development in check. He knew which lawmakers to rub shoulders with and was not shy about expressing his feelings. Legend has it that as a series of condominiums was being developed along Crescent Beach, just south of St. Augustine, Gamble left his mark by relieving himself onto one of the building's foundations in front of some startled onlookers.

Gamble maintained a warm relationship with his childhood friend Bruce McEwan and McEwan's wife, Margaret Lynne, known as M.L. Gamble joked he would always remember M.L.'s name—Margaret because his first wife was Maggie and Lynne because his daughter's name was Lyn. Bruce McEwan was a staunch Republican who served in the Florida legislature as a state representative from District 38 in Orlando from 1980 to 1992. While their careers took very different paths, the two remained close and loyal to each other. Gamble communicated with McEwan on legislative issues. Meanwhile, the McEwans would try to catch Gamble's performances and visit with him whenever possible.

As a traditional folklorist, it was only natural that Gamble formed relationships with folk pioneers and activists on the national scene like Pete Seeger and Stetson Kennedy. Gamble and Seeger performed together at folk festivals and shared a mutual admiration. In a video tribute to Gamble, Seeger recalled a time the two performed together at the Jonesboro Storytelling Festival in Tennessee. Seeger was in the middle of playing a Will McLean song when he forgot the lyrics. "Gamble came up close and gave me each line I needed so I could finish the whole song," Seeger said. "I'll never think about Gamble Rogers without thinking about how completely unexpectedly he helped someone out. I don't think any of us who ever knew him will ever forget him."

Gamble also sought out the company of Stetson Kennedy, the author and activist best known for having infiltrated the Ku Klux Klan in the

1940s. Kennedy hosted Gamble at his legendary Beluthahatchee residence in North Florida. It was at this same rustic setting that Woody Guthrie worked on his autobiography, *Seeds of Man*. The residence is designated as a literary landmark by the Friends of Library USA.

There were any number of creative projects as well. Gamble always seemed to be working on something. While he never received a film credit for his strolling musician's role in the 1964 horror flick *2,000 Maniacs*, he did receive cover billing in the critically acclaimed country music documentary *Heartworn Highways*. Filmed in late 1975, the documentary features performances from country music icons Guy Clarke, David Allan Coe, the Charlie Daniels Band, and a young Steve Earle. The cult classic serves up an intimate portrait of musicians at the root of the outlaw country music movement, including a behind-the-scenes peek at the hard-drinking, prolific singer-songwriter Townes Van Zandt.

Gamble appears in the film with a live performance of his story "Charlie's Place," chronicling the escapades of Harvey, "a commode-hugging drunk," and Marita, "a young woman of sporting morality" who had been "drummed out of high-rolling society" in Phenix City, Alabama. It's the same story that a few years later would feature Penrod and Elfrieda as its main characters and take place inside the Terminal Tavern. The changes are an example of how Gamble was constantly tweaking his stories, characters, and settings until he felt he got it right.

In *Heartworn Highways*, Gamble segues right from his comical monologue into a musical salute to Jack Daniels with his original whiskey-drinking, light-hearted lament "Black Label Blues," a fitting inclusion for a documentary about country music and Tennessee whiskey. "Black Label Blues" was always a crowd favorite. Folksinger Rod MacDonald, who sometimes opened for Gamble, recalled how on occasion there would be a tray of Jack Daniels shots nearby in response to the song's refrain, "Jack Daniels, if you please."

"When he'd finish," MacDonald said, "he'd pick up one of the shots and kind of dip his tongue into the edge of it and put it back down. He didn't drink any of it. I later found out he really didn't drink at all. He was a complete teetotaler. It was ironic that he would sing this song and everybody would want to buy him a drink." Rather than go to waste, Gamble would offer up the untouched shots to the audience between sets, MacDonald said.

Heartworn Highways, originally popularized through word of mouth, was one of the few recorded performances of Gamble Rogers available for public viewing during his lifetime and for many years after. A fortieth-anniversary limited-edition box set of the film and soundtrack was released in 2016.

Notwithstanding his grueling performance schedule, Gamble continued to explore ways of expanding his artistic boundaries, including his dedication to writing. He created a series of projects for NPR that included a play entitled *Good Causes: The Confessions of a Troubadour*, which aired on NPR's *Earplay* program in the winter of 1977.

In a letter to Nancy while on the road in Detroit, Gamble included an excerpt from a letter he sent to the program's producer, John Madden. Gamble detailed his personal vision for the play, which gives insight into his own goals as an artist and performer.

> This musical narrative should be a kind of documentary of Southern consciousness. I see it as incorporating songs from tradition, as well as songs of my own. There will be "formal" monologues of a comedic, whimsical satiric or dramatic nature, as they apply. I hope to establish early on that the listener is dealing with a specific type of narrator—one who is both a pilgrim and a professional troubadour. I would wish to come across as an observer of human nature in both a missionary and professional sense, that is, one who searches out impressions of Southern culture and who attempts to render up a polarizing sense of these impressions as popular art, art which instructs as well as entertains.

During the mid-1970s and early 1980s Gamble made guest appearances on both American and Canadian public television programs. He wrote the theme song for a PBS series on the Philadelphia Folk Festival and narrated several films.

While his various creative endeavors were well received, particularly in the realm of public radio and public television, there were no signature commercial successes, which, at least outwardly, seemed of little concern to Gamble. He was committed to the causes he deemed important.

He was also committed to staying true to his friends. Gamble's inner circle may have been tight, but he cast a wide net. Even some he met only once by chance left thinking he was their new best friend. There seemed little Gamble wouldn't do for a friend in need.

Dave Dowling, a musician, teacher, and videographer, met Gamble in St. Augustine in the early 1980s. "He had charisma," said Dowling. "I know a lot of people who, without even opening their mouth, have a presence about them."

Dowling owned a record store called Old Favorites that sold instruments, tapes, and CDs and had a small stage. One day Gamble approached Dowling about doing a benefit concert in the music shop for his ailing friend Jim Ballew, a singer-songwriter and environmental activist. It was common knowledge in music circles that Ballew was a hemophiliac. "They gave him some blood that wasn't checked out too well, and he was going to die," Dowling recalled. "People knew he was a hemophiliac, but nobody knew he had AIDS, which was a real bad word back then."

Because the benefit wasn't going to generate a payday, Gamble didn't want his manager to know about the concert, Dowling said. "It goes back to the old adage It's better to ask for forgiveness than permission," Dowling said, quoting a phrase Gamble often used in his performances. Gamble opened the show for Ballew, who then performed his own set inside the jammed-packed music shop. Ballew died in 1987 at the age of forty-three.

Dowling and Gamble also shared a close personal relationship with the luthier Paul Berger. The frail, diminutive Berger was a master craftsman who required a lot of personal attention. He had trouble keeping up with his bills and often landed in jail for any number of reasons, including DUI and failing to report to his probation officer.

"Paul is about the only person I know who could get ticketed for DUI riding his bicycle," recalled Jim Carrick. A fellow inmate described Berger as "nothing but breath and bones."

"It wasn't that Paul didn't have any business sense. He just didn't care," said Dowling. His life revolved around working on guitars, and there was no doubting his skill as a brilliant craftsman. Before moving to Florida, Berger worked for the Martin guitar factory in Pennsylvania, where he fixed guitars for the likes of Elvis Presley, Paul McCartney, Johnny Cash, and Merle Haggard, among others. It was at Gamble's urging that Berger moved to St. Augustine.

Berger had somehow managed to secure a stash of Brazilian rosewood before the precious wood was listed as endangered. His plan was to build a series of Gamble Rogers custom-designed guitars. The first prototype was still being developed when Gamble drowned in 1991.

It was not unusual for Gamble to appear in court or at the county jail on behalf of one of his St. Augustine friends who had run afoul of the law. On one occasion, Gamble, Dowling, and a few others went before a county judge to secure an early release for Berger who had been jailed for having a suspended license and failing to report to his probation officer. Berger's pro bono lawyer was there along with a group of character witnesses. After patiently listening to a few testimonials, the judge announced he had heard sufficient evidence to release Berger from jail. There would be no need for any additional speakers.

The judge then paused for a moment and said, "However, I look across the room and I see Gamble Rogers sitting there. All these years, I've had to pay money to hear Gamble talk. And I am not going to turn down a chance to hear him speak for free in my courtroom!" Of course, Gamble proceeded to wax eloquently, Dowling said. "I only wish we would have had a tape recorder."

22

SAM PACETTI SAT QUIETLY IN A LOFT overlooking the serenity of Salt Run in St. Augustine, not far from the historic lighthouse. The accomplished musician, approaching the age of forty, was at once contemplating the act of personal sacrifice and the collective unconscious as he began quoting the works of the philosopher Arthur Schopenhauer and the mythologist Joseph Campbell. Ultimately his thoughts turned back a quarter of a century to Gamble Rogers, his musical mentor who gave him lessons in folksinging and life from the very house on Magnolia Drive where Pacetti was now renting a second-floor apartment. It was no small irony.

"His actions, the way he lived his life, spoke of a person that was invested in the deepest type of moral code and in his subtle understandings of the nuances of human character," Pacetti said. "Gamble was equally at home talking to the cosmologist, the nuclear physicists, the doctor, the lawyer, the homeless man on the street. It made no difference. They were all given the same presence of his attention. It was the thing I viscerally understood when I met him."

They met in 1990 when Pacetti was a tenth-grader in high school. Gamble had come to the school to promote an upcoming appearance at the burgeoning St. Augustine Folk Festival. At age fifteen Pacetti was already a skilled guitarist, having been classically trained. He had gravitated to the Merle Travis and Chet Atkins style of finger picking. Although only a teenager, he was a Gamble Rogers fan and set out to meet the folksinger.

The day before his promotional appearance, Gamble came to the school to check out the sound system.

"I had strategically positioned myself in the auditorium because I knew he was going to be there," Pacetti said. "Much of my pattern in high school was to skip classes and go into the auditorium and play the guitar."

The two met briefly at the sound check. When Gamble arrived the next day, before his performance Pacetti asked if he could play something on Gamble's vintage 1939 Martin guitar. He offered up a few verses of "Goodbye My Bluebell," a Civil War song recorded by Merle Travis. Pacetti played it in the distinctive Travis style of guitar picking. Gamble was impressed. After completing his promotional performance at the school, Gamble approached the young guitarist.

"He asked if I would be interested in getting together to play some guitar," Pacetti recalled. "I didn't know what to think."

They arranged to meet at Gamble's house on Magnolia Drive. The first order of business was that Sam's father needed to size up his son's new folksinging mentor.

"I watched my dad fall in love with Gamble," Pacetti said. "Again this is what he was capable of doing. He didn't have to make a presentation. His person was his presentation. He had such authenticity about his being. If you were in any way perceptive, you got that."

What ensued were weekly sessions at the Magnolia Drive house, where Pacetti learned about the passing on of the folk tradition and a lot more. In his upstairs work room, Gamble maintained "the book," as Pacetti referred to his collection of music and notes. "It was like a holy grail to him. It had everything in it," Pacetti said. Gamble would bring out albums from artists who were important to him like Michael Smith, Steve Goodman, and John Prine.

The guitar lessons gradually evolved into an education on musical heritage and ultimately into "things you will need to know if you pursue this course of action." Life lessons. "Gamble was aware there were certain areas that I would need to give attention to," Pacetti said. "He told me I was good but that didn't mean anything. I had talent, but what's far more important was integrity. Here's what you are going to need to know along the way."

To shepherd him along, Gamble put his young protege in proximity to others in his circle like Bob Patterson and Jim Carrick. "He somehow knew I was going to need some guidance," Pacetti said. The lessons continued for a full year, right up until the week that Gamble tragically drowned. They would last a lifetime.

The house at Magnolia Drive was more than a place for guitar lessons. It was a refuge for Gamble and his family and an intimate gathering place for his closest friends. It was, in many ways, his much-needed inner sanctum after lengthy road trips from which he would return exhausted. It was also his own personal architectural landmark, which he was forever tweaking with an eye toward design perfection.

Gamble purchased the house in the mid-1970s shortly after beginning his romance with Nancy. Almost immediately he began transforming the inside of the house to reflect his own taste and architectural influences. Bob Parsons and Billy Qualls were two St. Augustine carpenters who spent years interpreting and implementing Gamble's vision.

Parsons met Gamble through Nancy, whom he had known from a previous construction project. When he built the first partition in the house, Gamble asked him how much he owed. "Well, you owe me forty dollars," Parsons said. "How about eighty?" Gamble replied.

"He was always like that," Parsons recalled. "No matter what I said, he always wanted to give me twice as much. He started me on a path of not just being a carpenter but a craftsman." He and Gamble spent hours looking over and discussing detailed drawings. Every square foot was given careful thought. The warm wood throughout the home set the tone. This became a house in which all would feel welcomed. There were built-in cabinets, ceiling treatments, and angled corners. There was great attention given to symmetry, especially in the windows.

Parsons, Qualls, and others worked on the house for the better part of ten years. "We'd be working on something and Gamble would call us from the road and change it," Qualls said. "Frank Lloyd Wright was his major influence. He loved his work."

With all the time they spent working on the house, Parsons and Qualls became firsthand observers of life inside the Magnolia Drive residence. There were family celebrations and gatherings, regular jam sessions, and a constant flow of guests. Kids and dogs roamed freely.

"I think he was just trying to create a big community of family and friends," Parsons said. "He was the kind of person everyone brought their problems to and he always had the time to talk. He was usually late going to where he was off to because there were people constantly wanting his time. I remember him flying out the door to get to the airport or the next performance."

More than just the house carpenters, Parsons and Qualls became immersed in life at Magnolia Drive. Parsons moved in next door.

"Gamble was like a second dad to me," Parsons said. "He taught by the example of the way he lived his life, so much so that I often found myself asking, What would Gamble do?"

Qualls spent hours with Gamble on the water, where he seemed the most at ease. If Gamble shared a passion equal to his love of guitars, it was boats. Gamble loved boats. He loved to build them and loved the hours he spent traversing Florida's waters, alone or with his family or closest friends.

The grassy backyard of the Magnolia Drive residence overlooked Salt Run, where Gamble launched his kayak or other water vessels. The place became known to locals as the Little Beach and was part of a tapestry of memories for Gamble's granddaughter Neely.

In a high school essay, written just before the ninth anniversary of her grandfather's death, Neely wrote poetically of her memories of the Magnolia Drive home.

> All my summer days were spent with my sister and my grandparents on Magnolia Drive. The water-colors danced on my paper as I painted with the rhythm of my grandfather and his friends playing the guitar upstairs. Sometimes I would run upstairs to ask if I could sit and listen while he played or just toiled with the notes that would soon become his intriguing works. After a while, I would ask him to play something for me. "Puff the Magic Dragon" would fill the room. Lying on the bed with eyes closed, I would picture the story as I heard the words, sang as naturally as breathing. If I close my eyes, I could picture them now.

Jam sessions at the Rogers residence were legendary. There was no telling who might show up on any given night. There was Dale Crider, Bob Patterson, Red Henry, Will McLean, and Jim Carrick. Also among the regulars were Gamble's neighbors, the musical couple Lis and Lon Williamson, who rented a house across the street.

Lis heard about Gamble from Evon Streetman, an internationally known photographer and artist who befriended Gamble early in his career. Streetman met Lis during the summer of 1976 when she was teaching at North Carolina's Penland School of Crafts in the Blue Ridge Mountains.

"She had all these hot guitar licks," recalled Lis Williamson. Streetman said she had learned them from Gamble and encouraged Lis to introduce herself to the folksinger if she was ever in St. Augustine. She took Streetman's advice and met Gamble at the Tradewinds a few years before she and Lon moved to St. Augustine in 1978.

When they rented their house on Magnolia Drive, they had no idea Gamble was their neighbor.

"One day we looked out our window, and we saw Gamble slingblading the grass in his front yard," Lon said. It was the beginning of a close personal and musical friendship.

Like Parsons and Qualls, Lon Williamson also helped work on the Rogers residence. "He would just sketch out these ideas for us in his office," Lon recalled. "His hands were so good." Gamble seemed to always be working, even when he was home. "He had a serious work ethic," Lon said.

As neighbors, Lis and Lon Williamson were intertwined with the Rogers family and Gamble's music. "His kindness to others, the way he conducted his life, was a lesson to us in our musical lives," Lis said.

In addition to the Magnolia Drive house jam sessions, the closeknit group of musicians sometimes assembled at the nearby Lighthouse Park for a picking party. And there were frequent sojourns across the Bridge of Lions to watch Gamble perform at the Tradewinds.

On one particularly rowdy night, Lon Williamson asked Gamble why he kept coming back to the Tradewinds after all those years. "It's good for me," Gamble replied. "I get a standing ovation at Carnegie Hall and get my ass kicked all over the stage at the Tradewinds."

"I guess he felt it kept him in check," Lon said.

For his part, Gamble did his best to bring the musical giants like Doc Watson, who influenced his life, to St. Augustine and the Tradewinds.

Lis and Lon said the iconic Watson was equally fond of Gamble. At a backstage meeting at Merle Fest in North Carolina, Watson told the Williamsons he had offered his own advice to the Florida troubadour. "I told Gamble to slow it down and clean it up," Lon recalled Watson saying.

Lis, Lon, and the other musicians who frequented the Rogers house played a significant role in perpetuating Gamble's legacy long after his untimely death, which no one saw coming except for maybe Gamble himself.

IV

Troubadour Emeritus

23

My father was a voyager.

—Gamble Rogers

On October 28, 1990, Gamble's father, the noted architect James Gamble Rogers II, died of natural causes at the family home at Temple Grove in Winter Park, Florida. He was eighty-nine. He had officially retired from full-time work ten years earlier, jokingly telling friends he was cutting back to forty hours a week. At the time of his death he was considered one of Florida's most respected and influential architects. His works helped define the landscape of Winter Park, Rollins College, and the surrounding communities.

The conflict over Gamble's career choice to forgo the family business had long since subsided. There was more than just mutual love and respect between Gamble and his parents. His father had been a great influence, introducing him to music and instilling in him a love of the outdoors and a passion for boats. Gamble never forgot his architectural heritage. He shared his father's dedicated work ethic and love for good craftsmanship. His mother, Evelyn, had given Gamble the example of southern gentility, a feature that became his signature quality both off and on the stage. While they might have preferred that he would have chosen the family business, Gamble's parents had come to an appreciation that he had followed his heart and was living the life he wanted. Occasionally they attended his performances. When Gamble knew his parents were in the audience, it was said he would tone down his act out of respect.

Delivering the eulogy for his father in 1990, Gamble spoke poetically and prophetically.

When he was forty-three years of age and I was six, my father and I stood alone in the early evening on a boardwalk at Cape Hatteras and watched an Atlantic Northeaster looming. A thunderhead nosed down along the horizon from the north as smooth and ominous as the snout of a macaw. A single star strove above a thunderous chaos of sky, shivering of timbers underfoot.

"Buckshot, did you ever think about what would become of you if you were out there by yourself in something like this?"

He faced the raging ocean and he radiated a strange power.

"What I mean is," he went on, "do you have any idea where you would go?"

I was terrified and felt I had been caught desperately wanting. I imagined I might be swallowed up. I feared even his power. But his voice was soft, his hand so meek upon my shoulder that I held to his leg as those words came back over me: "Do you have any idea where you would go?"

Suddenly he seemed to be asking the question for himself, and in that scant instant I went from the fear of strange powers to the most perfect love a man can share with another man, the love a son feels for a father who wholly declares his own confusion in the face of that dull mystification which is the levee of all mankind.

And so, my father was a voyager. I think of him now as on that ocean and shall ever see him in that striding star. I sense his elbow at the tiller, his hand on the lifeline, his finger on the string.

My father was a voyager.

Gamble Rogers, 1990

Less than a year after delivering the eulogy for his father, Gamble Rogers would come face to face with another raging sea, this time off the coast of Flagler Beach, Florida, where, in an instant of selfless sacrifice, he would pay the ultimate price.

24

~~~~~~~~~~~~~~~~~~~~~~

We all knew someday, the way the Gamble Rogers story
would end is that he was going to die some heroic death.

—BOB PATTERSON

SEVEN MONTHS AFTER DELIVERING his father's eulogy, Gamble emceed a musical tribute for his close friend Will McLean at the May
1991 Florida Folk Festival. McLean died from cancer a year earlier at
age seventy. The Black Hat Troubadour was widely recognized as the
father of Florida folk music. His influence on Gamble was significant.
Together they were the embodiment of the Florida folk scene. McLean
was credited with authoring hundreds of songs and was the recipient
of the Florida Folk Heritage award the year before his death. A passionate conservationist, McLean's ashes were scattered over the Ocklawaha
River.

McLean's death left Gamble, at age fifty-four, the last surviving
member of a quartet of closely knit folksinging giants who ushered in
a renaissance of Florida folk music in the 1970s and '80s. Jim Ballew,
the musician and environmental activist, died in 1987 at the age of
forty-three, losing his battle with AIDS, which he contracted from a
blood transfusion. A year earlier Paul Champion, the banjo master and
Gamble's longtime picking partner from the early days of the Baffled
Knight, died in a Gainesville hospital waiting for a heart transplant. He
was forty-six. Gamble helped spearhead fund-raising efforts for both of
his ailing musician comrades prior to their deaths.

In a four-year span, Gamble lost his father and three musical soul mates with whom he shared the stage and an appreciation of Florida's folk heritage. Each, with his own unique style of musicianship and songwriting, had made lasting contributions. Collectively, they garnered a spirit that defined the Florida folk movement near the end of the twentieth century.

Little did anyone know that Gamble's tribute to Will McLean in 1991 would be his last appearance at the Florida Folk Festival. The next year his peers and proteges would be offering their own tributes to Gamble from the Old Marble Stage on the banks of the Suwannee River.

Gamble spent part of 1991 getting his personal affairs and effects in order. He had custom drawers built inside his Magnolia Drive residence to chronologically organize his tapes and videos. "He went about organizing everything he had," said Jim Carrick. He sold his beloved Mercedes. When Carrick asked him why he replied, "It's time."

The signs were there. "Yep, he knew," Carrick said.

Sam Pacetti agreed. "It is my suspicion he most likely had a premonition of what was coming, because he started taking action that indicated that," he said. "One of the big ones is he took out a large life insurance policy on himself for Nancy. He was, in a very short period of time, starting to rapidly organize things that were loose ends."

The teenage Pacetti had become Gamble's special project in the months leading up to the folksinger's death. Their weekly lessons accelerated. Gamble began to seek Pacetti out when looking to escape from any number of social gatherings he had been coerced into attending. "He would call me and say he'd rather be playing guitar. Let's get together," Pacetti said. "Here I was so completely ignorant. There were probably a half a dozen times I opted out on an opportunity of spending time with Gamble, thinking this was going to be here for years, not understanding."

The last three times they met, Pacetti said he noticed a discernible shift in Gamble's personality. It was akin to being stern. He wanted Pacetti's full attention. "Gamble had this look when he wanted you to pay attention, where the world kind of collapsed around you," Pacetti said.

As Pacetti was about to head home on his bicycle from what was to be his final lesson, Gamble stopped him in the front yard of the Magnolia Drive home. Gamble put his hand on his student's shoulder and said, "You know, you really don't need to worry about the future or what's coming. You're going to do all right."

The conversation felt odd to Pacetti. "I knew something seemed awry." Pacetti recalled. "He then gave me a wink and said he'd see me next week."

Shortly before his death, Gamble unexpectedly ran into his child-hood friend Bruce McEwan on an airplane bound for Charlotte, North Carolina. When the plane landed, McEwan asked Gamble to join him at the US Air Club, where McEwan retreated straight for the smokers lounge. Gamble admonished the cigar-smoking legislator, telling him, "McEwan, you are going to die an early death." To which his longtime friend replied, "Jimmy, I'm going to outlive you by a long shot." Two weeks later, Gamble would be dead.

In the months leading up to his death, Gamble reportedly spent some time attempting to reconcile personal issues in his life that had taken their toll over the years. With stepchildren from two marriages and daughter Lyn from his first marriage to Maggie, he was often con-sumed with balancing the needs of his growing family, which now included grandchildren. There were tensions, to be sure.

"It had been tough on different members of the family," said Lyn. "I think he was trying to make amends." Gamble told his daughter he had finally made peace with Maggie years after their divorce. "He told me they had a wonderful conversation."

Late in the summer of 1991, Gamble visited Lyn, who was living in Birmingham, Michigan, and had recently given birth to Gamble's granddaughter Meghan. "He couldn't hold her enough, he just loved her so much," Lyn said. "I remember thinking that my entire relation-ship with him had just changed and how I could now give back to him. I was so happy to be able to give him a granddaughter."

However, as he left in the rental car for the return to airport and his flight back to Florida, Lyn had her own premonition.

"I walked out to the end of the sidewalk with Meghan and watched him drive away," Lyn said. "I went back into the house and cried, of course, because I missed him. But somehow I felt it was the last time I was going to ever see him."

They would speak again, one last time. On the Tuesday before his death, Lyn and Gamble had a lengthy, heartfelt phone conversation. She said nothing of her premonition, but the phone call was memorable. "It was God's way of preparing me for the shock," Lyn said.

Inside Gamble's home, next to the telephone, was a yellow note pad. He liked to doodle little drawings and notes while he talked on the phone. As he departed for a weekend camping trip with Nancy, he left behind what was to be his final note on the pad next to the telephone. Among the tiny spirals and scribbles he wrote, "So much to do . . . no time left."

25

As fate would have it, Gamble Rogers had the opportunity to perform at a music festival instead of camping at Flagler Beach State Recreation Area in early October 1991. Folksinger Frank Thomas had been working with organizers of a fall festival in Brevard County that included the noted novelist Patrick D. Smith, who authored the award-winning book *A Land Remembered*.

"They were trying to get Gamble to come down and perform," Thomas said. "I guess they were dealing with Charley and they were having trouble getting together on the price, so Gamble never did make it to the festival."

Gamble's manager, Charles Steadham, painfully acknowledged the failed negotiations.

"If there was one date in my life I wished I would have booked . . . ," Steadham recalled, his voice tapering off. "They really wanted Gamble, but they didn't have any money. I was trying to keep price parity. Gamble would have gone. He and I talked about it, and he supported me in turning it down. The only way you get the money up is to have a price point below which you won't go."

Steadham has lived with the regret ever since. It was one of two dates the Gainesville-based agent said he would like to have back.

There's one date in my career I wished I hadn't booked where a boy was hurt. I had nothing to do with it, but I'd give anything if I hadn't booked that date. It had nothing to do with me, but it changed lives forever. So, if I could change two dates in my entire career of booking, there's one date I would not have booked and there's one date I would have. Money would have had nothing to do with it. I had solid professional reasons for doing what I did in both instances, but I can assure you that if I had them to do over, I'd do them exactly opposite of what I did. I wouldn't have booked one and I would have booked Gamble.

As a result, Gamble had a rare free weekend. In the previous month he had been booked in Albany, Georgia; Philadelphia; Peekskill and Saratoga Springs, New York; and Knoxville, Tennessee. Another heavy road schedule awaited him.

He decided to spend the long, free weekend camping and bike riding with Nancy while visiting some of their favorite Florida locales. He invited along their friends attorney Sid Ansbacher and his wife, Cindy, to join them. He even hoped some of his children might join up with them over the weekend.

Ansbacher, an environmental attorney, had met Gamble about a year earlier and was representing a group of residents from the Little Beach neighborhood in their opposition to a dock being built on Salt Run.

"Gamble was involved because he was a kayaker," Ansbacher recalled. "He didn't believe a large dock was consistent with the neighborhood open use of the Little Beach." While it was ultimately determined the dock was permissible, the group succeeded in having it constructed so as not to encumber the view or access to Salt Run.

Like so many others, Ansbacher soon found himself drawn into Gamble's world. They shared a love of reading, especially the classics. "He had an amazing library," Ansbacher said, noting that the singer's bookshelves included Faulkner, Steinbeck, and "the usual suspects."

Of particular interest was a semi-obscure book entitled *Rommel and the Rebel*, by Lawrence Wells. The fictionalized military adventure was one of Gamble's favorite books, Ansbacher said. "I have no idea what intrigued him about it," he said. "I've read it four or five times. There must be a key."

For the long weekend, the group planned to make camp at the Flagler Beach State Recreation Area just off the US A1A coastal highway. On the itinerary was a series of day trips and bike rides to some of their favorite sites, like Boulder Beach at Marineland and Washington Oaks Gardens State Park.

Following a morning bike ride on Thursday, October 10, they decided to grab lunch at a beachside place known as Snack Jacks on the southern end of Flagler Beach. After lunch they returned to their campsite.

Seemingly out of nowhere, chaos ensued. Ansbacher remembered emerging from a restroom to a scene of utter desperation. Nancy was standing on the bluffs staring out at an angry ocean of wild whitecaps. There were park rangers on the scene and onlookers in what seemed like a state of panic. As he tried to comprehend the situation, Ansbacher suddenly realized there was no sign of his wife, Cindy. There was also no sign of Gamble.

Moments earlier, a terrified teenager had come running in frantically from the beach screaming that her father had been caught up in the wild surf and was being carried out to sea. Without hesitation Gamble blew up his nearby air mattress and stripped down to a button-down shirt and his underwear. He headed straight for the ocean in the direction of the drowning tourist. Ansbacher's wife, Cindy, an accomplished swimmer, also headed out to join the rescue effort.

The undertow was overpowering. Park Ranger Chuck McIntire was an experienced swimmer familiar with the Flagler Beach surf. He was friends with Gamble and Nancy, which is one of the reasons they chose to camp at the Flagler Beach park. McIntire, too, headed out into the rough surf. At one point he encountered Gamble, who was still gripping his raft, signaling he was OK. Cindy Ansbacher, however, had been caught up in a churning sea and was being pulled down by the undertow. McIntire grabbed her wrist and pulled her onto the shore. "She was very shaken and weakened," Sid Ansbacher recalled. "She told me later she was literally about to go under for the last time when Chuck grabbed her wrist and pulled her in. He saved her life. There's no other way to put it."

After being assured his wife would survive the near-drowning, Ansbacher went to find Nancy, who was standing halfway up the bluff that bordered the shoreline. They were looking for some sign of Gamble on his raft. From that vantage point, beyond the breakers they saw the unmistakable. "There was Gamble, face down out in the water," Ansbacher recalled. "It was pretty clear at that point he had died."

Since it was early October there were no lifeguards on duty. A volunteer on a wave runner brought Gamble's body back to shore. There are conflicting versions as to whether anyone tried to provide CPR. "The belly was bloated at that point . . . he had clearly drowned," Ansbacher said.

A rescue team also pulled to shore the body of the deceased Canadian tourist, forty-eight-year-old Raymond Tracey of Tecumseh, Ontario. In an instant, two lives unknown to each other had been inextricably linked in death.

It was a sudden yet heroic end for Gamble. There would be no final performance, no farewell tour, no chance to say goodbye to friends and loved ones, no chance to finish his work. It was all over in the blink of an eye. The water had always been so much a part of his life. Now, it took the life from him.

It was not the first time he attempted to rescue someone from the water. Bob Patterson recalled that Gamble had pulled a struggling swimmer from the chilly current at Ichetucknee Springs in North Central Florida years earlier. This time was different. This was a dangerous sea. Gamble knew his physical limitations. But in the moment it didn't seem to matter.

"Gamble could not turn his head beyond about a forty-five-degree angle," said Sam Pacetti, referring to his mentor's spinal condition. "He had to rotate his entire body to do so. So he knew he couldn't swim. That was obvious, but I don't think that thought even entered his mind. It was just that there was this human being in duress."

While many of Gamble's friends expressed wonder as to how they might have reacted under such circumstances, it was clear they understood Gamble's response.

"He had no choice," said Jim Carrick.

For all the discipline Gamble displayed in his life, it didn't come as a total shock to Ansbacher that he would throw caution to wind and head straight for the wild surf. "He was a very gentle soul and was very measured," Ansbacher said. "In many ways he carried a lot of the architect genes in him. He did a lot of 'measure twice, cut once' in his life. Yet, he would do the damnedest things." Among them was his refusal to wear seat belts, something Ansbacher was surprised to learn during the course of their camping trip. "Nancy said they considered seat belts to be too constraining," Ansbacher recalled. It was part of the confounding complexity and contradiction that defined Gamble's life and ultimately his death.

Still, the idea that it would all end so suddenly was unthinkable, especially for a man who seemed to possess such capacity for living life to its fullest. News of the tragedy would send shock waves of disbelief and grief throughout the folk community. For Ansbacher, it was a surreal, dark day that he compartmentalized. He has rarely spoken about it in public but did offer a reflection.

> Going back to that day, so many people say he was taken from us too early. I've candidly thought that given his arthritis, whether it's expedient to say or not, he still had most of his powers. How would Gamble have been had he continued to deteriorate and not been able to do the things he loved, the woodworking, the kayak work, the guitar work? In some sense, I've comforted myself by thinking maybe because he lived so much in the slightly over fifty years he was given that in some ways it may have been a blessing that he didn't suffer more. I feel guilty for thinking that, but I still to this day wonder.

For the bereaved Nancy, there was only the consolation that Gamble had gone first.

"I'm just relieved it was him before me," Nancy told her daughter Stephanie the night of his death. "No one would take care of him or worship him like I do."

26

~~~~~~~~~~~~~~~~

Voyager upon life's sea.
To yourself be true.
And where'er your lot may be,
Paddle your own canoe.

—SARAH T. BOLTON, "PADDLE YOUR OWN CANOE," 1853

WORD OF GAMBLE'S DEATH traveled through the folk community like a bad dream. For some, it was one of those moments forever etched in the annals of time.

"It's like Where were you when John F. Kennedy got shot?" recalled Bob Patterson. When Patterson received the call from one of Gamble's stepdaughters, he froze in stunned disbelief. "I recall vividly all of a sudden being in some kind of a vacuum. I remember thinking, 'Not now. Wait a minute, the story's not over with yet.' It was like somebody pulled the plug. It was dreadful."

Patterson met the grief-stricken family members at the funeral home. Gamble was still lying on a gurney. Patterson, hesitantly, went in to say goodbye to his friend. "It was like looking at a cocoon. It didn't even look like him. It was surreal. I hadn't even fully realized what I had lost."

With legal assistance from others, Nancy was able to sidestep the normal state requirement for an autopsy, sparing Gamble what she deemed an unnecessary indignity. "He [expletive] drowned," she said.

In the hours following the tragic events at Flagler Beach, Sid Ansbacher took his wife, Cindy, to a local hospital for observation after her near-drowning. He eventually ended up with Nancy back at the Rogers home on Magnolia Drive, where he began the painful task of calling some of Gamble's family and friends.

"It was then I realized the magnitude of Gamble's relationships when I saw the names of some of the people I was calling," Ansbacher said. "The 'Chet Atkins' of the world and so on. I discovered, not to my surprise, just how many people would have listed Gamble as one of the two or three most significant people in their lives at the time that he died. What an honor and privilege it was to share any time with him. It was horrible the way it ended."

For Gamble's children, his death was shattering. He not only served as the father to a daughter and four stepchildren, he was the moral compass that held things together as best he could in two families split by divorce.

His stepdaughter Lolly was working in St. Augustine at the Zanzibar Restaurant, owned by Lis and Lon Williamson, when she received the call. "I just went in the back of the restaurant and hid," said Lolly. "I remember just being frozen. I was in shock."

News of Gamble's death spread quickly, delivering an unfathomable blow to his dedicated inner circle, many of whom learned the devastating news from each other. Dave Dowling called Jim Carrick. Carrick, in disbelief, called his contacts with Flagler Beach Rescue who confirmed the tragic news. Carrick, in turn, called Sam Pacetti, among others.

"I sequestered myself for a little bit and went through my process," Pacetti said upon hearing the news. It was at that moment that the enormity of Gamble's sudden loss registered with the teenage guitarist, who asked himself, "What did I miss? What might I never know? What experiences will no longer be there?"

Pacetti spent the evening camped out in Carrick's boat, on dry land, with their mutual friend Tom Jenkins as they tried to console each other. Throughout the late afternoon and early evening, word descended on the ancient city of St. Augustine. Solemn faces gathered outside Gamble and Nancy's house on Magnolia Drive. A few blocks away, across the Bridge of Lions, the Tradewinds Tropical Lounge began filling up with patrons longing perhaps for one last performance that was never to be.

Charles Steadham was producing a two-night show for IBM in Raleigh, North Carolina, when he received a call from his office that Gamble had drowned. "I was devastated," Steadham said. "It was so totally unexpected."

The impact on Steadham was profound. "I find it easier to discuss the passing of family members," he said. "There's just something about losing Gamble and the way we lost him and knowing the influence he had on so many people. Everything I did after meeting him was influenced by him. I try my best every day of my life to think about what Gamble would have done in certain situations, but I come up short time and time again."

Several of Gamble's friends reported having a similar mysterious dream in the days following his death.

"In the dream I was standing on the riverbank talking to him," Carrick said. "I asked when was he thinking about crossing, and he told me, 'Tomorrow night, in my boat.' At the time I had no idea what he was talking about."

It wouldn't be long before Carrick and others would find out the meaning behind this seemingly strange, mysterious dream.

27

IN THE AFTERMATH OF HER SUDDEN LOSS, one of the first calls Nancy Rogers made was to Gamble's close friend Harvey Lopez. She called with a very personal request. She wanted Harvey to build Gamble's casket.

Lopez was another of the colorful figures in Gamble's inner circle. An accountant by trade, the affable Lopez moonlighted in a popular North Florida band known as Catfish and the Hush Puppies. He also shared Gamble's passion for wooden boats. Gamble, along with friends like Lopez and Bob Patterson, loved to build boats and tinker with them as needed.

Lopez recalled a time he was working on one of Gamble's favorite boats, a Thompson runabout. After about forty minutes of Lopez' craftsmanlike attention fixated on the boat's stern, Gamble leaned over with his patented wry grin and proclaimed, "Harvey, we're not building a Steinway."

Lopez had experience working on boats. But he had never built anything resembling a casket. Nevertheless, the call for help came. It set in motion what Lopez and others like to call "the folk process," people helping out whenever they are needed. You just don't say no. It was a creed Gamble lived by.

To assist with the casket, Lopez called on two friends with experience in boat building and cabinetry, Jesse Allen and Brad Kinsey. Their first task was to round up enough Florida cypress to build a coffin.

"When we first got started, I looked over at Brad, who was about six foot five, and realized he was too tall," said Lopez. "I was certainly too short, so I turned around and said, 'Lie down, Jessie.'" They then proceeded to trace the measurements on a workbench, figuring out the various details of Gamble's coffin as they went along. It was only natural that the casket took the shape of a boat. "We had to get the measurements just right so it would fit properly into the cement vault," Lopez said. The casket's unconventional shape required special dispensation for burial.

With less than three days to the funeral, Lopez, Allen, and Kinsey worked around the clock, giving attention to every detail including polishing the brass handles taken from a decommissioned minesweeper and staining the cypress wood with an old rosewood finish. Meanwhile, to accommodate a viewing at the funeral home, Nancy purchased a traditional casket for Gamble, just so there could be a viewing while his burial casket was being prepared.

It was the only casket Lopez ever built. "It's not something you want to get good at," he said. When Gamble's "boat" was ready, the woodworkers wrapped the casket in sheets and delivered it to the funeral home in the back of Lopez' pickup truck. The music playing in the truck's cabin on the ride over was "Keep on the Sunny Side," Lopez said.

When they returned to the funeral home the following day to fasten down the top, Lopez slipped in one final item, a handmade, three-foot oar. "You have to have a paddle to cross the river," Lopez mused.

Gamble was buried in an Irish linen white shirt with silk threads, handmade by Nancy. When talking about impending death Gamble often quipped, "One more white shirt'll do ya." He was also buried wearing his ostrich-skin cowboy boots. The casket was lined with silk from Nancy's wedding dress. In the casket was a note written by his eight-year-old granddaughter, Neely.

Dear Grandpa,
I miss you.
I brought you some flowers.
I really hope you like them.
I feel that you are with me.
But I also feel you are missing.
Our family misses you very very much.

I try to remember good times.
But sometimes I can't help thinking about bad ones.
Thanks for takeing me to Georgia
I am sorry if I spell words wrong.

The burial took place in Gamble's hometown of Winter Park, attended mostly by family and a few of his closest friends.

Following the burial, the first of several public memorials was held on October 20, 1991, at the Lighthouse Park in St. Augustine only a few blocks from his home on Magnolia Drive. More than three hundred people attended the memorial service, which included an impromptu jam session with many of Gamble's friends performing under the sprawling oaks. The Tradewinds Tropical Lounge ran ads in the local paper noting it would be closed during the memorial service and would reopen later that day. In the months that followed there would be similar tributes and memorials throughout the state, including more ceremonies and concerts in St. Augustine, in Gainesville, and at the 1992 Florida Folk Festival, which was dedicated to Gamble's memory.

The memorials bore witness to Gamble's reach beyond his core of regular followers. Total strangers appeared, seemingly out of nowhere, to tell tales of how a single performance or a particular song had changed their lives. Even more telling were the unfamiliar faces of individuals who had been the anonymous recipients of Gamble's kindness.

At one of the memorials, a gentleman approached Gamble's daughter Lyn at the end of the receiving line. "Gamble was my best friend," he told her. "I didn't recognize the man, so I asked him to tell me more," Lyn said. The man was from the Tri-County area in North Carolina and had been in the technology business when he fell upon hard times. He lost his job, and one thing led to another until he became homeless and was living under an overpass. His only contacts were others in his homeless community with the exception of a single friend who would check on him regularly and provide him with medication and food. One day the friend took the homeless man to hear some music at a local club in the hopes that it might raise his spirits.

"Daddy was playing at the club and while he was warming up, the friend introduced the homeless man to him," Lyn said, recalling the story. "He was disheveled and dirty, but Daddy took a real interest in him and wanted to know his story."

After the show Gamble came back to the homeless man and asked if it would be all right if he called some of his contacts in the technology business. The homeless man was startled. "Look at me. I'm filthy and homeless. Why would you do this?" he asked.

"Daddy apparently made arrangements to get him a hotel room along with some food and clothing," Lyn said. "A few days later he was contacted by someone in the technology business who offered him a job. As it turned out, the job was at IBM, where he met his wife and was still employed."

Tributes to Gamble would continue to pour in for years after his death. Charles Steadham remembered a call he received from a man saying he had to talk to someone about what Gamble had meant to him. "He said he never met him and only saw him perform once," Steadham recalled. "Thousands of people [were] in front of the main stage at the Kerrville [Texas] Folk Festival, and he was in the back of the crowd. He said that performance by Gamble spoke to him over the heads of that audience. The goodness and sincerity of the man on stage spoke to him in such a profound way that he credited it with turning his life around. By the end of the call, we were both in tears."

It's the stuff on which legacies are built, a process that began almost immediately after Gamble was laid to rest in a boat with an oar, ready to cross the river.

28

Gamble Rogers was a troubadour in the ancient
and traditional sense of the word.

—NANCY LEE ROGERS, LETTER TO THE FLORIDA ARTS COUNCIL, 1993

GAMBLE ROGERS'S DEATH sent his family and friends into a spiraling tailspin as they searched for ways to cope with their sudden loss. Bob Parsons, his neighbor and friend, said he just "shut down" for awhile as if the world had stopped. Jim Carrick recalled a similar emotion.

Many of Gamble's musical companions like Michael Peter Smith, Charley Simmons, and Larry Mangum found their expression in song, composing moving tributes and ballads to their lost hero.

For his grieving widow, Nancy, the path ahead was clear—keep Gamble's spirit, memory, and music alive, most especially for the people of Florida. In the weeks following his death she was inundated with tributes and remembrances from across the country.

"It came sweeping in from all sides, from far and wide," she wrote in a letter to friends a month after his death. "It held me up, and held me together and propelled me forward. Gamble's legacy came resounding back and is infusing us all, again and again, with all the qualities he brought out to us in his life, inspiring us at every turn to do our very best, to be more than we ever dreamed we could be."

With the assistance of state representative Bruce McEwan, attorney Sid Ansbacher, and state senator Bill Bankhead, she set her sights on having the state park in Flagler Beach where Gamble died renamed in his memory. She explained her reasons in her letter to friends.

> He loved the land everywhere he went, it delighted him. To say to all, in our day and time lived someone very special; not a warrior or a killer of men, but a man who spent his life in creative pursuit and enriched and inspired everyone he touched and continues to do so for all who remember him. We need a monument like that, to speak to us and for us and for our time and to leave a lasting message of hope for all those to come.

Despite opposition from some local authorities in Flagler Beach, the 1992 Florida Legislature unanimously enacted a bill establishing the Gamble Rogers Memorial State Recreation Area at Flagler Beach. The new law read,

> WHEREAS, James Gamble Rogers IV was born on January 31, 1937, in Orlando Florida, grew up in Winter Park as the son and grandson of prominent architects, and was a long-time resident of St. Augustine, and
> WHEREAS though Gamble Rogers studied creative writing at Stetson University and architecture at the University of Virginia, instead of designing buildings and houses, he pursued as his life's work the writing and singing of songs, the telling of stories, and the making of music, and
> WHEREAS, over the years Gamble Rogers developed a national reputation as a musician, appeared on national radio and television shows, produced albums and tales of his songs and stories, and in his native state earned the title of "Florida's Troubadour," and
> WHEREAS Gamble Rogers was a true son of Florida who, in his songs, stories and music, focused on the flora, the fauna, and the plain folks of Florida, the state he loved, and
> WHEREAS, Gamble Rogers, an outdoorsman, a conservationist, and protector of Florida's natural environment was, with his wife, Nancy, an avid camper whose favorite area was the park and beach at Flagler State Recreational Area, and
> WHEREAS, on October 10, 1991, Gamble Rogers drowned while

attempting to save the life of a Canadian visitor who was struggling in a violent tidal current at the Flagler Recreational Area, and WHEREAS, Gamble Rogers enriched the hearts and lives of thousands of Floridians and others with his music, his mirth, his spirit, and his love of Florida and gave to all who heard him perform a profound sense of the uniqueness and special nature of his home state, NOW THEREFORE,

Be it enacted by the Legislature of the State of Florida:

SECTION 1. THE FLAGLER STATE RECREATIONAL AREA IN FLAGLER COUNTY IS HEREBY RENAMED THE GAMBLE ROGERS MEMORIAL STATE RECREATION AREA AT FLAGLER BEACH.

The sprawling 144-acre state park is situated on a barrier island bordered by the Atlantic Ocean to the east and the Intracoastal Waterway to the west. It is known as a prime nesting beach for three species of turtles and offers visitors a variety of swimming, kayaking, hiking, and camping opportunities. A simple bronze monument mounted on stone on the park's ocean side is dedicated to Gamble Rogers, Florida's Troubadour, "Beloved Guitarist, Storyteller, and Gentleman."

The park consistently boasts the highest occupancy rate of any state park in Florida and doubled the number of its camping sites in an expansion project completed in 2015.

There have been attempts by a handful of city officials to have the park's name revert back to the original Flagler Beach State Recreation Area. In 2013 a city commission task force, citing local economic impact, voted to recommend that the Florida legislature give the park back its original name. Their argument was that putting emphasis on the Flagler Beach name would attract more tourists to the area. Besides, they argued, most people didn't know much about Gamble Rogers. The recommendation was later dropped after a community backlash and when it became apparent the state legislative delegation had no intention of changing the name. The *St. Augustine Record* newspaper called the attempt to remove Gamble's name from the park an "act of cultural heresy."

The naming of the state park in Gamble's memory was only one of Nancy's many endeavors to preserve her husband's legacy. She helped coordinate tribute concerts around the country and assisted with fund-raising for the Nature Conservancy, Gamble's favorite charity.

Her dream was to establish a real Oklawaha County on land that had been rescued from the proposed Cross Florida Barge Canal project. In her vision, the Oklawaha County nature preserve would house a small Gamble Rogers museum and an environmental education facility.

While that dream never came to fruition, there would be other significant memorials, including the naming of a middle school in St. Augustine, the establishment of an annual folk festival, and Gamble's induction into the Florida Artists Hall of Fame.

The legacy would not come without its challenges.

29

NANCY ROGERS WASN'T ALONE in her diligence to preserve Gamble's legacy.

The Gamble Rogers Memorial Foundation was established in 1992 as a not-for-profit corporation by Gamble's family and friends. In addition to serving as a living memorial to Gamble and his work, the foundation was established to "promote interest, knowledge and appreciation of Florida folklife and rural heritage by encouraging and facilitating the presentation, collection, study and preservation of customs, crafts, music, literature and oral traditions and histories."

Among the foundation's purposes was "to make grants or gifts of money or other property for scholarships, for research and for any activities deemed appropriate for the increase in knowledge and appreciation of Florida folklife and rural heritage."

The foundation, recognized as a tax-exempt 501(c)3 organization, is housed in the Gainesville offices of the Blade Agency, the entertainment booking agency owned by Gamble's longtime agent and manager, Charles Steadham, a founding director of the foundation. Inside, there is a room devoted to an extensive collection of Gamble Rogers's archives. The foundation maintains a website, GambleRogers.com, and markets and sells Gamble's recordings and videos.

Certain tensions surfaced in the years following the singer's death between Steadham and some of Gamble's inner circle, including Nancy.

At the time of his death, none of Gamble's recordings were in circulation. While he had released three albums, all were out of print. Another live performance had been recorded but had yet to be released.

There were no CDs, tapes, or recordings available to the public. Some people, including Nancy, wanted to blame Steadham.

For his part, Steadham felt he was devising a long-term plan to centralize the distribution of Gamble's works and protect them for future generations. "Since Gamble's death, I've felt right or wrong, the most important thing was to try to reassemble that entire body of work and position it where it was protected in one place over time, over the next several generations," Steadham told the *Gainesville Sun* in 1994.

In the same *Gainesville Sun* article, Nancy accused Steadham of stalling. She was particularly unhappy that Gamble's final album, a live recording entitled *Oklawaha County Laissez-Faire*, remained unreleased three years after Gamble's death. "It's gone on too long," she told the newspaper. "Three years . . . you could build the Eiffel Tower in three years."

Steadham meanwhile focused on acquiring the various masters from Gamble's recordings at his own expense and eventually acquired the intellectual property rights to all of Gamble's works. Over time he painstakingly built an extensive library of archives and released a complete catalogue of Gamble Rogers CDs and a live DVD performance, all of which are distributed exclusively through the Gamble Rogers Memorial Foundation. The foundation's website features a comprehensive compilation of information about Gamble Rogers, including video clips, articles, tributes, and even a detailed description of the mythical Oklawaha County and its residents. Steadham also invested considerable time and resources into making a full-length documentary about Gamble's life.

Despite any perceived differences over the release of Gamble's recordings, Steadham, Nancy, and others worked together tirelessly in the early 1990s to preserve Gamble's legacy. There were any number of posthumous awards, including the National Storytellers Lifetime Achievement Award, the Kiwanis Award for Bravery, and the Carnegie Medal for Heroism.

Among his supporters' most passionate efforts was a campaign to have Gamble's name enshrined in the Florida Artists Hall of Fame. The hall was established by the Florida legislature in 1986 to recognize individuals who have made a significant contribution to the arts in Florida. The early inductees represented a who's who list of artistic giants such as Ernest Hemingway (1987), Marjorie Kinnan Rawlings (1987), and Tennessee Williams (1989).

Nancy, with the assistance of Steadham, McEwan, and others, made it her personal mission to see Gamble inducted into the hall. In doing so, she composed a tribute to her late husband that described his artistry and influence and gave context to his recognition as Florida's favorite troubadour. In a 1993 letter to the Florida Arts Council she wrote,

> Gamble Rogers is a Florida legend, in the hearts of Floridians and in the eyes of the world. Everywhere he went, all over this country and Canada, he was 'The Florida Troubadour.' With his courtly manners, handsome, dignified bearing, his vivid vocabulary and insightful humanist humor, he was the embodiment of the best the South has to offer.

> Gamble Rogers was a troubadour in the ancient and traditional sense of the word. The troubadour was the original performing artist, and, Gamble was one of the remaining masters of the art. The troubadour travels from community to community bringing people together and elevating and transporting them with his artistic power, weaving a web of creative sharing across the land. The work of the troubadour is not spectator art, it is experiential. People often brought their children to see Gamble's shows, not simply to share an evening of music and laughter, but for inspiration and challenge to give them a living, breathing model and hero.

> This is the magic that Gamble Rogers worked everywhere he traveled and this is especially true in his home state. Gamble created a Florida mythology, a set of stories, insights and definitions that gave Floridians a sense of identity, tradition and kinship that is invaluable in today's dispossessed world, in this immigrant state. The people of Florida need to keep his spirit alive in their memories, in their history and in their traditions and legacy.

Author and activist Stetson Kennedy penned his own letter in support of Gamble's nomination to the Florida Artists Hall of Fame.

"I was privileged to know Gamble both personally and professionally, and it is my opinion he has had few if any equals as a creative contributor to the cultural and artistic life of the State of Florida," Kennedy wrote. "A living tradition in his time, Gamble Rogers's contributions will unquestionably live on to enrich the lives of future generations not only in Florida but throughout the nation."

Like so much else, recognition for Gamble did not come easy. His first nomination before the Florida Arts Council in 1993 fell short of the required vote. His supporters like Steadham and others did not give up easily. Jimmy Buffett, who himself would be inducted to the hall in 2000, wrote a ringing endorsement of Gamble in 1995, telling the Florida Arts Council, "I personally know of no one who better exemplified what it means to be a Florida artist than Gamble Rogers."

It took time, but the persistence paid off. Finally, in 1998, Gamble was voted into the prestigious Florida Artists Hall of Fame. Meanwhile, in St. Augustine work was under way to establish an annual folk festival designed to keep the music and spirit of Gamble Rogers alive for generations to come.

30

ONE OF THE FIRST SCHEDULED APPEARANCES on Gamble's calendar following his death was the St. Augustine Folk Festival on October 25–27, 1991. Gamble was a mainstay for the St. Augustine festival that was held in the city's original amphitheater. The 1991 festival, held only two weeks after his death, unexpectedly turned into a tribute to his life and his music. Similarly, the 1992 Florida Folk Festival in White Springs was dedicated to Gamble's memory.

Folk festivals had been a part of Gamble's performing life almost from the beginning. He debuted at the Florida Folk Festival in 1963, long before he had attained any significant recognition. Gamble was, as much as anything, a true folklorist. He recognized the value and importance of these festivals. Unlike college campuses and performing halls, folk festivals were artistic happenings where folk art came to life in a variety of expressions juxtaposed over a two- or three-day event usually held in a scenic outdoor setting. It was here that the folk tradition, in song and practice, was celebrated and passed on to the next generation. Gamble reveled in this opportunity to perform with his contemporaries and to introduce new artists to the folk scene.

There were certainly better-paying gigs, but Gamble knew his important place and influence at these annual gatherings. He made them a priority and was a featured headliner at festivals throughout the country. It was only a matter of time before a music festival bearing his name would be established.

The Gamble Rogers Folk Festival had its roots in the dedication ceremony in 1994 for a new middle school being built in St. Augustine on US Highway 1. Teachers and staff from various schools in St. Johns

County conducted a contest to name the new school. A student from the R. J. Murray Middle School in St. Augustine submitted an entry for the name Gamble Rogers Middle School. The name was selected by the county's school board over several other entries. The board's chair, Sharon Hatsell, told the *St. Augustine Record* that Gamble's life "provides a good role model for pupils."

At the urging of Dan Downs, a teacher at the new school, a dedication ceremony was organized featuring Gamble's close friend Bob Patterson and other musicians. With the demise of the St. Augustine Folk Festival after Gamble's death, the idea was hatched to establish an annual folk festival linked to the new middle school bearing Gamble's name.

On May 4–5, 1996, the first Gamble Rogers Folk Festival was held at the St. Augustine Amphitheater. The festival was organized by Downs, Patterson, and the school's principal, Jim Springfield, an avid Gamble fan who was appointed to head the school in 1995. The first concert was sponsored by Gamble Rogers Middle School and its Parent-Teacher Organization.

"Gamble Rogers was an entertainer but more importantly he was a man of character and principles," Springfield wrote in the inaugural souvenir program. "This is a way of life we hope our students learn during their time at the GRMS. Teaching is not the task of the school only, it is the responsibility of the entire community. Therefore as you talk to children about Gamble, and other role models, speak openly of the positive, so they can learn what you value."

The first festival was intended to help fund a section of the school's library dedicated to Florida history. Gamble's widow, Nancy, helped provide the vision for the library and assisted with the funding, according to the festival's inaugural souvenir program. The festival was an all-star lineup of Gamble's friends and proteges. Among them were Patterson, Michael Peter Smith, Sam Pacetti, Don Oja Dunaway, Frank and Ann Thomas, Jim Carrick, Dave Dowling, Dale Crider, Charlie Robertson, Nigel Pickering, and Lis and Lon Williamson. There were workshops, tributes, and a jam session finale.

The initial event was a success and began a run that has continued for more than twenty consecutive years. During its peak, the festival became such an attractive venue that performers were turned away due to an overflow of musical acts wanting to participate. Headliners have included Arlo Guthrie, Jim Stafford, and Richard Thompson.

The concert's organizers, including Patterson and Paul Linser, a developmental biologist with the Whitney Laboratory for Marine Bioscience, have emphasized the festival's connection to Gamble. Each year there is an "I Remember Gamble" contest in which participants pay tribute in song or storytelling.

The contest has inspired such moving musical tributes to Gamble as Larry Mangum's "The Last Troubadour" and Charley Simmons's "Song for Gamble."

The festival, a 501(c)3 tax-exempt entity separate from the memorial foundation, has also given a stage to the next generation of folk artists who never knew Gamble but were moved by his spirit. One such performer, Mike Lagasse of the Wild Shiners, helped organize a 2014 Gamble Rogers tribute CD called *Oklawaha County Jamboree*, featuring young performers covering Gamble's songs. Lagasse never met Gamble. He knew of him only from stories he heard over the years. "I wanted to make a CD that would, in some meaningful way, connect Gamble's fans and friends, his songs and a younger generation of musicians together," Lagasse wrote in the booklet that accompanied the CD. The project was funded in part by the crowd-sourcing platform Kickstarter and was produced by Gamble's longtime friends and neighbors Lis and Lon Williamson at Gatorbone Records.

Still one of St. Augustine's premier events, Gamble Fest has been challenged in recent years with inclement weather, venue changes, and fluctuating attendance. In an attempt to broaden its exposure, an annual concert series was added to help with funding. The festival also presents a weekly radio show on Flagler College radio entitled *Radio Free Oklawaha County*, which features music from performers at the May festival and is hosted by concert organizer Paul Linser and Mike Lagasse.

In recent years, Gamble's daughter Lyn, granddaughter Meghan, and stepson Chuck have performed at the festival. His first wife, Maggie, also attended several of the festivals. It was moved from the sprawling amphitheater setting to the more intimate Colonial Quarter in downtown St. Augustine. Gamble's granddaughter Neely began taking an active role on the festival's administrative team.

Despite the various noble attempts at preserving his legacy, Gamble Rogers still remains a virtual unknown to much of the general public outside of St. Augustine. Years after his death, his recordings are difficult to come by in music stores or on popular online applications. All of his recordings are available through the Gamble Rogers Memorial Foundation and can often be found at music festivals in Florida.

With the passage of time some of Gamble's most vocal and visible advocates have passed on. Nancy spent the years after Gamble's death committed to perpetuating his memory. But her life after Gamble was marred with hardship. She was embroiled in a family dispute over portions of Gamble's estate, in which she prevailed. Nancy was stricken with a rare, horrific form of skin cancer called mycosis fungicides lymphoma. The disease ravaged her once-vibrant body and shrank it to a mere seventy pounds. She died in 2005 at the age of sixty-one.

Bruce McEwan, Gamble's earliest friend, passed away at age eighty in November 2017 during the editing of this book.

As of this writing, his most passionate surviving supporters pressed forward. Jim Carrick continued performing weekly gigs at the Tradewinds Tropical Lounge, almost always with a Gamble tune or two in his set list. Bob Patterson remained active on the folk scene and as a committed environmental advocate for Florida's endangered waters and streams. Like Gamble, Patterson took a serious interest in helping promote the careers of young folk artists, imbuing them with a sense of purpose behind their work. The surviving members of Gamble's inner circle like Dale Crider and Charlie Robertson were never shy about paying homage to Florida's troubadour when given the opportunity. But their numbers are shrinking, and as Patterson said, "I'm not getting any younger."

There is concern that one day Gamble Rogers will be forgotten by all but a few, his memory washed away much like his earthly presence that ended in a turbulent sea.

Even the middle school named in his honor has had issues perpetuating his legacy. Jim Carrick recalled that Gamble's prized Guild guitar was among the personal items on display inside a case in the school's lobby. After a few years, the guitar was in need of some upkeep. Carrick volunteered to have the guitar cleaned and take care of any repairs. His offer, repeated on several occasions, went unanswered for an extended period. Frustrated, Carrick went to the school principal at the time and asked, "If you are not interested, who can I talk to?" The answer shocked him: "She said there had been some complaints. A lot of the teachers said they didn't like walking by a dead man's things every day."

Carrick, along with the school's former principal Jim Springfield, immediately arranged to have the guitar removed from the school. "We had already made our minds up that we were going to jail if we had to, but we were getting the guitar out," Carrick said.

Aside from a framed wall display on loan from the Gamble Rogers Memorial Foundation there is little connection between the middle school and its namesake. There is no longer an official affiliation with the annual music festival. Few if any school officials seem to know anything about Gamble Rogers. There are renewed efforts under way to reestablish a link between the school and the festival.

Unlike those designed by his architectural forefathers, there will be no grand edifices to give testament to Gamble's artistic talent. His extensive catalogue of whimsical stories and Southern Gothic songs will endure, but they were never created for their commercial appeal. At best, they were meant to be performed live so as to connect the artist to his audience. More than his body of work, it was Gamble's personal magic and spirit that his most ardent disciples hope to preserve.

As for Gamble, he would have most likely scoffed at the idea of a legacy.

"He probably wouldn't want a book written about him, wouldn't want a folk festival, a school or a park named after him," conjectured his daughter Lyn. "He would have said, 'Give it to the next guy.'"

He was far too humble for such a fuss. Instead he would have been content and at peace, in the words Agamemnon Jones, "to let his work speak for itself."

Epilogue

It's a humid, sticky night at the University of Florida's Whitney Laboratory for Marine Bioscience, nestled across the street from what was once North Florida's most popular tourist attraction, Marineland.

On this particular Saturday night, a group of mostly gray-hairs has assembled inside the laboratory's Lohman Auditorium to hear legendary Chicago folksinger Michael Peter Smith. He has just finished a touching yet humorous performance of "Palomino Pal," a cowboy fantasy dedicated to his childhood idol Roy Rogers, when he begins to talk quietly about another Rogers—Gamble Rogers, no relation to Roy.

"Gamble was as close to being perfect as you can get," Smith said. "Everybody loved him. And he was so cool. I've spent the last twenty-two years trying to be as cool as Gamble. I'm still trying."

Smith then proceeded with "Gamble's Guitar," his poignant tribute to his good friend whose heroic end unfolded off the coast of Flagler Beach only a few sandy miles from where tonight's concert is taking place.

> Whole lot of country, whole lot of blues
> Whole lot of sunshine, sand in your shoes
> Sound of a player who paid his dues
> Put some miles on that Mustang car
> Shot of Merle, jigger of Chet
> Little bit of Will McLean I bet
> Only the wind in the palms and yet
> I thought I heard Gamble's guitar

In the hushed auditorium you can hear a pin drop.

On the front row, Bruce McEwan, the former state legislator and Gamble's childhood friend, gazes skyward, his eyes moist with tears as the song continues.

> I want to sleep beside the sea tonight
> Hear the crash of the waves, the tops all white
> I want to be grateful for what's gone right
> I want to wish upon a star
> God bless old friends that have gone before
> Bless old banjos and old country stores
> Bless old Florida forever more
> And God bless Gamble's guitar

It's been more than a quarter century since Gamble Rogers's death. Yet in Florida, along the eastern coast, and in pockets throughout North America his name strikes a visceral chord.

There is a mystery as to why so many were so deeply affected by Gamble. To be sure, there were other fingerpickers more skilled. His voice was smooth but not necessarily distinct. His stories were hilarious commentaries that resonated with common folks. They were, as Gamble said, stories that celebrated an "Arcadian lifestyle" of truck drivers and fishermen. But he connected with intellectuals just the same. His songs were deep, emotional, and often dark. The Faulkner influence was undeniable. Yet in all his years of performing and recording, he never had anything close to a commercial hit. So how did he connect so deeply with his audience and loyal followers?

"It's tempting to wrap your brain around who he was," said his daughter Lyn. "But he was so multifaceted and he brought so many things to the table in an unassuming way."

Somehow through the wry smile, the eye squint, the chiseled chin, and the stiff back emerged a southern gentleman of high integrity. It came through embedded in the sorry tales of Still Bill and Neon Leon. It pierced through his Southern Gothic laments of "Alabaster Sally" and "The Girl from Stony Lonesome." Gamble Rogers was the real deal, and his audiences and followers intuitively knew it.

"He's about as close as you get to the real thing," said the popular comedian and musician Jim Stafford. "As a human being, he stood taller than most people."

It's a theme that echoed beyond the strings of his Guild guitar.

More than ten years after Gamble's death, Charles Steadham received an unexpected email from Taiwan. It was from a fan who had seen Gamble perform in Canada, most likely at the Mariposa Folk Festival in Toronto. He was requesting that the entire catalogue of Gamble's CDs be shipped to him overseas. "His music brought me pleasure, and his integrity made me want be a better human being. I wish to continue this joy and desire," the fan explained in his email.

"All of his stories and songs were amazing, but it pales in comparison to who he really was," said stepdaughter Lolly Rogers. "He was a humanitarian, and he had an uncanny ability to reach someone that needed to have comfort. He was able to do that naturally, without any judgment, to be there for someone."

In a 1993 letter to the editor of the *St. Augustine Record*, a restaurant dishwasher offered the following perspective:

> Gamble Rogers on occasion ate at the Lighthouse Restaurant where I worked as a dishwasher. He was always surrounded by friends. His fame as a musician and storyteller was well known by all.
>
> Coming from the hot kitchen for a cold drink, sweat pouring down my body, I happened to look up and notice a man gazing intently at me. He didn't look away when our eyes met. He reminded me of a wise old man yet still looking for more. In that brief moment when he was taking my measure, I not only saw intellectual curiosity but also a friendly inviting man to know and be known. It, of course, was Gamble Rogers.
>
> I never met the man. I'll never forget the look. He was interested in strangers enough to give his life for one.
>
> P. S. BERESH, ST. AUGUSTINE.

Gamble didn't require the trappings of commercial success. It was his autonomy and authenticity that spoke to his audience and those around him. "He was intelligent enough to know that things he may have walked away from would not have been the life for him," said

Sam Pacetti, Gamble's student and protege. "Here is a man who led an exemplary life, and he afforded me a template of what it means to live with integrity."

Gamble's house on Magnolia Drive on Salt Run in St. Augustine remains with Nancy's family. At various times when they've needed refuge, Gamble's friends like Jim Carrick and Sam Pacetti have rented space in the upstairs loft. The electric bill from Florida Power and Light is still addressed to James G. Rogers, Gamble's legal name.

"I didn't really know that guy, the 'businessman' and his legal name and all the weight it carried," said his granddaughter Neely Ann Miller, who was eight years old when Gamble died. "I knew Gamble, the magical, creative, mysterious, humorous, and playful human. I saw magical things through the eyes of a child, and those are the only memories I have to draw from."

Even though she was too young to have experienced the full measure of Gamble, their relationship was special. She was blessed with a keen insight into his spirit and the ability to express it in her own words.

All accolades, fame, and fortune aside, he really was a soul that led other souls to be better, do better, dream bigger, laugh harder, and follow their passions. To follow their own unique soul. That is what Gamble did with his life. I believe the lesson and legacy left for us is simply to do the same. Do more of what you love. Do what your soul is most inspired by. Do what scares you. Do what's right, not what is easy. Let your soul shine and let it light the path, your true path, not one given to you by your legal name or legal baptism or past life dharma.

In historic Florida locales like St. Augustine's Tradewinds Tropical Lounge and the Stephen Foster memorial on the banks of the Suwannee River, there are those who still hear the distant sounds of Gamble's guitar.

God bless old friends that have gone before
Bless old banjos and old country stores
Bless old Florida forever more
And God bless Gamble's guitar

Acknowledgments

More than a quarter of a century after his heroic death, a biography on Gamble Rogers, Florida's troubadour, was long overdue. It might not have happened without the inspiration and assistance from some of Gamble's closest friends and family members.

At the top of the list was his childhood friend, the late Honorable Bruce McEwan of Orlando, who passed away during the editing phase of this book. He knew Gamble perhaps longer than anyone. He started my journey by introducing me to those who knew Gamble best. Bob Patterson served as the truth guru and spiritual guide throughout. I am deeply grateful to Jim Carrick, Sam Pacetti, Frank Thomas, Lis and Lon Williamson, Harvey Lopez, Larry Mangum, Michael Peter Smith, and M. L. McEwan, all of whom shared more than just their memories. To all those who graciously granted interviews, thank you!

To Gamble's family, I am grateful for your trust that allowed me the opportunity to shed some light into this very private artist and humanitarian who was so publicly revered. Special thanks to Jack Rogers, Maggie Rogers, Lyn Rogers Lacey, Lolly Rogers, Chuck Rogers, Stephanie Frost, and Neely Ann Miller.

To Charles Steadham, a very special thank you for your ongoing support, for granting access to Gamble's works, and for the permissions as cited in the author's note.

To Sian Hunter of the University Press of Florida, who believed in this story from the beginning, thank you for your support and patience. Thanks to Ali Sundook and the staff at the University Press of Florida for your help and guidance. Thanks also to those who helped read the drafts and offered advice—Tana Silva, Bob Kealing, Diane J. Diekman, Christopher A. Keese, Mike Goldman, and Bill Vlasic.

The State Library and Archives of Florida proved to be an invaluable resource. I am appreciative of the support and guidance provided by the archives staff.

Finally, much appreciation and gratitude to my family for their unconditional support and especially to my partner in life, Edith, who was with me for every single word of this project.

Gamble Rogers Discography

The Lord Gives Me Grace and the Devil Gives Me Style

Produced by Stephen Powers. Studio LP originally released 1977 by Mountain Railroad Records (MR 52779). CD re-released 1996 by Gamble Rogers Memorial Foundation, Oklawaha Records (OK1001).

Gamble Rogers Live: The Warm Way Home

Produced by Robin McBride for Bird Productions and Stephen Powers. Live LP originally released 1980 by Mountain Railroad Records (MR52786). CD re-released 1996 by Gamble Rogers Memorial Foundation, Oklawaha Records (OK1002).

Gamble Rogers / Home Grown Philosophy (Part One)

Recorded in 1984 before a live studio audience at WFSU-TV, Tallahassee, FL, as *Oklawaha County Laissez-Faire*. Produced by Charles Steadham and Bill Sykes. DVD released 2010 by Gamble Rogers Memorial Foundation, Oklawaha Records (OK2001V).

Sorry Is as Sorry Does

Produced by Robin McBride for Bird Productions. LP originally released 1986 by Flying Fish Records (FF362). CD re-released 2001 by Gamble Rogers Memorial Foundation, Oklawaha Records (OK1003).

Oklawaha County Laissez-Faire

Produced by Robin McBride for Bird Productions with Gamble Rogers. CD released 1996 by Gamble Rogers Memorial Foundation, Oklawaha Records (OK1004).

Signs of a Misspent Youth

Produced by Charles Steadham. CD released 1999 by Gamble Rogers Memorial Foundation, Oklawaha Records (OK1005).

Good Causes

Produced by Charles Steadham. CD released 2003 and re-released 2016 by Gamble Rogers Memorial Foundation, Oklawaha Records (OK1006).

Appendix A

Over the years, numerous tribute songs and ballads have been written in memory of Gamble Rogers. The three that follow represent a small sampling of those that have been performed as part of the "I Remember Gamble" program at the Gamble Rogers Music Festival.

"GAMBLE'S GUITAR"

Words and music by Michael Peter Smith, Bird Avenue (ASCAP), 1968

> Down in St. Augustine F-L-A
> I was walking along the beach one day
> Sun beating down like a steel drum plays
> So bright that you couldn't see far
> I was listening to the waves roll in
> Humming a tune from I don't know when
> Thinking about times that won't come again
> And I thought I heard Gamble's guitar
>
> I had a book and a joint and some chunks of bread
> For the seagulls wheeling above my head
> Elmore Leonard and Panama Red
> And the music from a distant bar
> I was thinking about a real good friend
> Feeling kind of sorry for myself just then

And a whole lot older than I'd ever been
And I thought I heard Gamble's guitar

Whole lot of country, whole lot of blues
Whole lot of sunshine, sand in your shoes
Sound of a player who paid his dues
Put some miles on that Mustang car
Shot of Merle, jigger of Chet
Little bit of Will McLean I bet
Only the wind in the palms and yet
I thought I heard Gamble's guitar

It sang of the snakes and swamps and the vines
Sang of the cypress and the phosphate mines
Nights up late in the whispering pines
Watching for a shooting star
Stony roads and fishing poles
Afternoons at the swimming hole
A mouthbow played by a Seminole
I thought I heard Gamble's guitar
In the old boys picking 'round the front porch stove
Digging for treasure in a pirate's cove
In a coffeehouse down in Coconut Grove
Doesn't matter where you are
Behind Spanish walls in Winter Park
In the smell of jasmine in the dark
Running a speed trap outside Starke
I thought I heard Gamble's guitar

Whole lot of country . . .

Where the sea breeze blows but there's still the heat
With a sunburned nose and sandspurs in my feet
At my high school sweetheart's in old St. Pete
And her husband's saying "Have a cigar"
Riding south past Manatee
Heading down to the Florida Keys
Getting things straight between Jesus and me

And I thought I heard Gamble's guitar
I want to sleep beside the sea tonight
Hear the crash of waves, see the tops all white
I want to be grateful for what's gone right
I want to wish upon a star
God bless old friends that have gone before
Bless old banjos and old country stores
Bless old Florida forevermore
And God bless Gamble's guitar

Whole lot of country . . .

God bless Gamble's guitar

"THE LAST TROUBADOUR (REMEMBERING GAMBLE ROGERS)"

Words and music by Larry Mangum, 2005

Yes, I'm among the lucky ones
Who lived to call him friend
This story of a traveler is a tale without an end
A life of love and music
No one could ask for more
Yes, I knew the Last Troubadour
In the Old City, I knew the Last Troubadour

If finger picks were knife blades and guitar strings made of wood
He would carve a work of art as only Gamble could
And if fantastic stories would open Heaven's doors
They were flying open when he played his last encore

Yes, I'm among the lucky ones . . .

Like a shuttle in an orbit 'round a world that he designed
He would fly just close enough to spin his yarns and rhymes
Then he'd head out to the next town
Where they thought he was their own
But we all knew the Troubadour
Would soon be coming home

Now who has lived the kind of life that they would choose again
Who is there among us that could count more friends
And who has left a legacy that will never end
No one but the Last Troubadour

Yes, I'm among the lucky ones . . .

"SONG FOR GAMBLE"

Words and music by Charley Simmons

I've walked the streets of Old St. Augustine
And I feel as though I'm halfway in a dream
Though memories stroll by on parade
Like some transcendental promenade
And Gamble played that old guitar

Charlotte Street just seems to make me blue
And it don't feel the way it did in '72
And I flash back to a time before
When those notes rolled out the Tradewinds door
And Gamble played that old guitar

I close my eyes, it takes me where
The smell of jasmine's in the air
And Gamble played that old guitar

He played this: [finger-picking guitar interlude]

Sang those songs and told those stories well
And we all laughed and cried
How could we ever tell
That he'd leave us on that sandy shore
Where we'd all long to hear once more
Gamble play that old guitar

Nowadays I've drifted far away
From that Ancient City where I thought I'd stay
But in my mind I oft return

To the place where the haints and the vandals turned
And Gamble played that old guitar

I close my eyes, it takes me where
The smell of jasmine's in the air
And Gamble played that old guitar

As long as I can draw a breath
I know I never will forget
When Gamble played that old guitar
When Gamble played that old guitar
When Gamble played that old guitar
I wish I could hear Gamble pick that old guitar
Like bubbles on a dolphin's breath

Appendix B

A TASTE OF GAMBLE ROGERS'S STORIES

Gamble Rogers was the consummate storyteller. While he stuck to a core of stories that seemed to work best, he was forever tweaking them on stage with subtle changes, ever mindful of the audience reaction. Many of his stories are preserved in written form, either in booklet notes for his CDs or in original files maintained in the archives of the Gamble Rogers Memorial Foundation in Gainesville, Florida. Below are two examples.

BOVINE MIDWIFERY

Bill is a consummate expert in the field of bovine midwifery. He has to be a good cow midwife because every one of those newborn calves is money in the bank for an agrarian entrepreneur like Bill. Bill had this old Bossie-cow, she was about to drop a calf. He heard her lowing out in the upper forty—that's the mud hole behind the chopping block—sounded like she was in hard labor.

He got a piece of rope, ran out to help her, got around behind her, first thing he noticed, it was a complicated birth because the calf had breached. He tried to turn the little fella around and get it coming out head first into the world the way Mother Nature intended, but he had no success. He had no recourse then but to take hold of the calf's hind legs and start in to pulling. That cow's tied to the tree lowing, Bill's pulling on that calf's hind legs.

Now, the interstate highway ran right behind the property at this point. Along comes this young woman with straight black hair and horn-rimmed glasses, driving a little MG, with New Jersey plates, smoking some non-domestic tobacco. Boogie, boogie, boogie, boogie, hmm. She looks down in the field and she sees Bill and the cow. She stops the car, she runs up there, she says "Sir, can I help you?" He says, "Yes ma'am, take hold of a leg and pull." They pulled, and they pulled, and that calf came out into the world healthy and capered away.

Bill said, "Ma'am, I'm much obliged to you for helping me out in my time of need. Now is there any way in which I can recompense you for the services you have rendered here?" She said, "No sir, Mister, I wouldn't take a nickel for that. I just want to ask you one thing." He said, "What's that, Ma'am?" She said, "How fast was that little one going when it hit the big one?"

Well, I'm sure glad we've got some country people in here tonight. I told that story in New York City and I got a whole roomful of blank stares.

James Gamble Rogers IV, *Gamble Rogers Songs and Stories*, © Steady Arm Music (BMI), 2006

PENROD AND ELFRIEDA

Nothin' too excitin' ever happened across the road at Charlie's, except when Penrod came in. Now, Penrod was a local, devout, deeply committed, totally involved, commode-huggin' drunk. He dealt mainly in small change—he'd steal hood ornaments off Peterbilt diesels at the A&W Root Beer parkin' lot and fence 'em at the Western Auto Store. . . . He'd dynamite catfish in copious, commercial quantities in the Little Econlockhatchee River and sell 'em in bulk to Howard Johnson's for scallops.

But he was chiefly celebrated among the populace of our community for having imported into our thankful midst a young woman of sporting morality by the name of Elfrieda, who had been drummed out of high-rolling society in Phenix City, Alabama, after her health card had been punched so many times it disappeared into thin air.

Now, this Elfrieda considered herself an interpretress of the modern dance, and lo, whenever the dulcet and mellifluous tones of Miss Peggy Lee were heard to resonate upon the Wurlitzer, singing that grand old American standard "Fever," Elfrieda would lose herself in an engaging series of peregrinations, pirouettes, and bumps and grinds calculated to leave even the most diffident of observers fraught with horn. On this particular night, Penrod and Elfrieda and a randy retinue of rednecks came stompin' into Charlie's. All the local good old boys were bellied up to the bar, snappin' the galluses on their Big Dads, their left hands upraised in that fervid type of mono digital articulation which bespeaks an argument in progress about the relative merits of post hole digging attachments for John Deere as opposed to Massey-Ferguson tractors. They turned about and beheld the entry of Penrod and Elfrieda, and in a great man-swarm gaggle of Arcadian underachievers, they slewed crabwise over the polished floor of that establishment, stokin' the juke with legal tender in such a manner that Peggy Lee's "Fever" played ninety-seven times. And Elfrieda so lost herself in a transcendental evocation of her timeless art, struggling gamely, as it were, up the Olympiad of her sensibility, that she shucked her duds right on Charlie's terrazzo floor.

I responded to this visual phenomenon of unslaked carnality by instantly proposing marriage to a one-eyed waitress who happened by. Oh, I didn't want to get into anything heavy! I just wanted to set up light housekeepin' in a pup tent out in the parkin' lot until closin' time. I was out there with my borrowed ball peen hammer and my steel tent stakes puttin' that tent up in the asphalt. Some idiot ran over my foot with a pickup truck, emptied his ashtray in my sleepin' bag—and the woman rejected me. So I had no choice but to go home and write this old song.

Well, I just wanted to tell you the true story so you'd understand where art comes from.

James Gamble Rogers IV, CD booklet notes for *The Lord Gives Me Grace and the Devil Gives Me Style*, © Steady Arm Music (BMI), 1996

Notes

Prologue

"When your work speaks for itself": James Gamble Rogers IV, *Oklawaha County Doctrines of Citizenship*, © Steady Arm Music (BMI), at Gamble Rogers Memorial Foundation, http://www.gamblerogers.com/stories/doctrines.asp.

Introduction

"We've lost Gamble": Frank Thomas, interview by the author, May 7, 2014, Lake Wales, FL.

"He couldn't swim in a swimming pool": ibid.

"He could relate to a fruit picker": ibid.

"In the final analysis": James Gamble Rogers IV, *Oklawaha County Doctrines of Citizenship*.

"Gamble was the greatest spirit I've ever known": Tom Paxton quoted in Nancy Lee Rogers to "Dear Friends," attachment, November 1991.

"You could have put his face as the marquee": Charlie Robertson, interview by author, February 5, 2014, St. Augustine.

"No one really knew who he was": "Erase Gamble Rogers' Legacy?" editorial, *St. Augustine Record,* November 7, 2013.

"What a crass tradeoff": ibid.

"Everyone wanted to play guitar like Gamble": Jim Carrick, interview by the author, December 12, 2013, St. Augustine.

When interviewed for the radio show: Frank Thomas, interview, May 7, 2014.

Part I. My Father Was a Voyager

Chapter 1

Joseph Hale Rogers was living on a fifty-acre farm: Jack Rogers, interview by the author, June 6, 2014, Winter Park, FL.

William Preston, then the surveyor of Fincastle County: "Joseph Hale Rogers," February 12, 2012, Find a Grave, https://www.findagrave.com/cgi-bin/fg.cgi?page=gr&GRid=84857045.

It seems Preston wanted . . . a trade: Jack Rogers, interview, June 6, 2014.

According to a Rogers family history: Mamie Williamson, *History of the Rogers Family* (Florence, KY: William and Anne Fitzgerald, 1958), 4–1, http://bcplfusion.bcpl.org/Repository/RogersFamily.pdf.

Family talk has it: Jack Rogers, interview, June 6, 2014.

James Gamble Rogers I was born in 1867: Patrick W. McGlane and Debra A. McGlane, *The Architecture of James Gamble Rogers II in Winter Park, Florida* (Gainesville: University Press of Florida, 2004), 1.

Among his most notable works was a series of buildings: "James G. Rogers Architect Is Dead," *New York Times*, October 2, 1947.

In 1915 John Arthur Rogers loaded his family into a Model T Ford: McGlane and McGlane, *Architecture*, 8.

His first attempt to attend Dartmouth College was put on hold: ibid., 12.

At Dartmouth, Gamble II set the intercollegiate time record: ibid., 13.

In addition to athletics and academics: Jack Rogers, interview, June 6, 2014.

It was at Dartmouth he attended a performance: ibid.

While en route: ibid.

Chapter 2

Once back in Daytona: Unless otherwise cited, details and background of family history in the chapter are based on Jack Rogers, interview, June 6, 2014.

Gamble II agreed to join the crew of the *Caprice*'s new owners: James Gamble Rogers II, untitled, unpublished essay, circa 1938, Winter Park.

"Fair weather with moderate to fresh east winds": ibid.

"We realized the absolute necessity": ibid.

Part II. Tales of a Misspent Youth

Chapter 3

"Want to guess who this is?": Bruce McEwan, interview with the author, February 16, 2014, Crescent Beach, FL.

Long before he was to establish himself: ibid.

The name Gamble Rogers III: Jack Rogers, interview, December 18, 2017, by phone.

"I guess it was pretty well assumed": Bruce McEwan, interview, February 16, 2014.

"He was a gentleman": ibid.

Initially the two boys lived in the house: Jack Rogers, interview, June 6, 2014.

The boys' mother, Evelyn, took an immediate interest: ibid.

The result was an arrangement: ibid.

"Needless to say": ibid.

The family moved into the small house: McGlane and McGlane, *Architecture*, 30–31.

"As kids we had a lot of freedom": Jack Rogers, interview, June 6, 2014.

"We had a lot more freedom at his house": Bruce McEwan, interview, February 16, 2014.

In spite of the freedom: Jack Rogers, interview, June 6, 2014.

When the events of World War II: McGlane and McGlane, *Architecture,* 32, 35.

"She didn't mind much": Jack Rogers, interview, June 6, 2014.

While she was not in the family business: ibid.

Among the stations they listened to: ibid.

"We were focused on reading, music, and storytelling": ibid.

"He could hear someone in another room": ibid.

"beguiling casement with alligator texture and silver clasps": Gamble Rogers, "Nine Pound Hammer," *Oklawaha County Laissez-Faire,* Oklawaha Records, Steady Arm Music (BMI), 1996.

Years later, as an established performer: ibid.

Jimmy started with the ukulele: Jack Rogers, interview, June 6, 2014.

If anything, he was somewhat modest and reserved: Syd Chase, interview by the author, March 2014 26, Mount Dora, FL.

The story's protagonist: Bruce McEwan, interview, February 16, 2014.

As the story goes, Hutto "pulled up adjacent to the teeming turkey pens": Gamble Rogers, "The Great Maitland Turkey Farm Massacre of Nineteen and Fifty-Three," *The Lord Gives Me Grace and the Devil Gives Me Style,* Oklawaha Records, Steady Arm Music (BMI), 1996; originally released by Mountain Railroad Records, 1977.

The Thanksgiving tale is included: Susan Stamberg, *Every Night at Five: Susan Stamberg's All Things Considered Book* (New York: Pantheon, 1982).

Saturday matinees: Gamble Rogers, "Saturday Afternoon at the Baby Grande," *Gamble Rogers Live: The Warm Way Home,* Oklawaha Records (OK1002), 1996; originally released by Mountain Railroad Records, 1980.

Trudy Butram: "Trudy Butram and the Immaculate Contraption," *Gamble Rogers Live: The Warm Way Home,* Oklawaha Records (OK1002), 1996; originally released by Mountain Railroad Records, 1980.

Eulalah Singleterry: "The Passion of Miss Eulalah Singleterry" *Gamble Rogers Live: The Warm Way Home,* Oklawaha Records (OK1002), 1996; originally released by Mountain Railroad Records, 1980.

As a teenager in Winter Park: Jack Rogers, interview, June 6, 2014.

In high school, it meant the end: ibid.

"More signs of a misspent youth": Gamble Rogers, "Saturday Afternoon," *Oklawaha County Laissez-Faire.*

He read just about anything: Jack Rogers, interview, June 6, 2014.

"If there was a harder way": ibid.

He was the senior class president: *Towayam,* Winter Park High School yearbook, 1955.

"Being the gentleman he was": Jack Rogers, interview, June 6, 2014.

"It was characteristic of him": ibid.

"He was a very proper gentleman": Joan Abendroth Pratt, interview by the author, June 23, 2015, by phone.

"He had zero patience with snobbery": ibid.

The night of the high school prom: ibid.

He was particularly taken with . . . Merle Travis and Chet Atkins: Jack Rogers interview, June 6, 2014.

Like other teenagers of the day he had been mesmerized . . . [by] Elvis Presley: Rowland Stiteler, "Gamble's Winning Bet," *Florida Magazine* (*Orlando Sentinel*), August 2, 1987, 10.

Chapter 4

"If you want to study philosophy": Gamble Rogers, "Bean Creek Alphabet," *Sorry Is as Sorry Does*, Oklawaha Records, Steady Arm Music (BMI), 2001; originally released by Flying Fish Records, 1986.

Originally populated by Native Americans: "Habersham County History," US GenWeb Project, updated July 11, 2010, http://www.rootsweb.ancestry.com /~gahaber2/history/history.htm.

Following the devastation: ibid.

Shelby Smith . . . was an established businessman: Lucian Lamar Knight, *A Standard History of Georgia and Georgians*, vol. 4 (Chicago: Lewis, 1917), 2197.

"He knew the men would be involved": Jack Rogers, interview, June 6, 2014.

"That's where a lot of the stories would come from": ibid.

From the time they were small children: ibid.

"It was kind of a dual existence": Lyn Rogers Lacey, interview by the author, November 18, 2014, Callaway Gardens, GA.

The farm inspired such youthful tales: Gamble Rogers, "The Sky Lake Campfire Girls," *Warm Way Home.*

"It was like the first time": ibid.

"Daddy and Pauline": Lyn Rogers Lacey, interview, November 18, 2014.

"The mystery and the spirit of the song": Jack Rogers, "Gamble Rogers Tribute at the 1992 Florida Folk Festival," May 24, 1992, Florida Memory, State Library and Archives of Florida, https://www.floridamemory.com/items/ show/237000.

"Far beyond Blood Mountain": Gamble Rogers, "Blood Mountain," *Lord Gives Me Grace.*

Pauline, the motherly cook: Lyn Rogers Lacey, interview, November 18, 2014.

Pauline was meticulous: ibid.

"The people up there were well known": Jack Rogers, interview, June 6, 2014.

As he gazed up at the carved initials: Lyn Rogers Lacey, interview, November 18, 2014.

Chapter 5

"Always dream and shoot higher": William Faulkner, "The Art of Fiction," *Paris Review*, Spring 1956.

His brother, also a student: Jack Rogers, interview, June 6, 2014.

"He'd had a few drinks": ibid.

During his first two years: Joan Abendroth Pratt, interview, June 23, 2015.

"I was serenaded as the sweetheart:" ibid.

"He was becoming more and more drawn": ibid.

"It really hampered his movements": ibid.

"It just wouldn't have been a good fit for me": ibid.

"I wouldn't say he had a checkered college career": Maggie Rogers, interview by the author, March 8, 2015, Mount Dora, FL.

"There were a number of areas of study I could have pursued": Gamble Rogers, quoted in Rowland Stiteler, "Gamble's Winning Bet," *Florida Magazine* (*Orlando Sentinel*), August 2, 1987, 11.

One of the more publicly circulated accounts: Jack Milne, interview by the author, March 6, 2014, Jacksonville, FL.

"Paul Berger invited my daughter": ibid.

"Every day Faulkner held regular office hours": Gamble Rogers, paraphrased by Milne, ibid.

What did happen next: Lyn Rogers Lacey, interview, November 18, 2014.

"He would basically chicken out": ibid.

"He had intuitively come to the place": ibid.

Maggie Rogers told yet another version: Maggie Rogers, interview, March 8, 2015.

"Faulkner influenced a lot of what he did": ibid.

He even paid tribute to the master: Gamble Rogers, "Airstream Trailer Orgy," *Sorry Is as Sorry Does*, Oklawaha Records, Steady Arm Music (BMI), 2001; originally released by Flying Fish Records, 1986.

He left the University of Virginia without a degree: Jack Rogers, interview, June 6, 2014.

In typical fashion, Rogers summarized: Gamble Rogers, "Orange Blossom Special (Finale)," *Oklawaha County Laissez-Faire*.

Chapter 6

"Read, read, read": in Emily Temple, "The Best Life Advice from William Faulkner," Flavorwire, http://flavorwire.com/331385/the-best-life-advice-from-william-faulkner.

Granberry was a close friend and confidant: "Edwin Granberry (1897–1988): English Professor and Noted Novelist," Golden People: Notable People of Rollins and Winter Park, Rollins College, http://lib.rollins.edu/olin/oldsite/archives/golden/Granberry.htm.

"I know James so well": Edwin Granberry to J. Ollie Edmunds, Stetson University, July 31, 1959, provided by Jack Rogers.

"I wouldn't be surprised": Jack Rogers, interview, June 6, 2014.

Born in 1938 in the Panama Canal Zone: "Biography," Remembering Paul Champion, http://www.paulchampion.net/biography.html.

A heart murmur discovered: Ronald Johnson, *North Florida Folk Music: History and Tradition* (Charleston, SC: History Press, 2014), 89.

A self-proclaimed bohemian: Dan Holiday, interview by the author, February 3, 2015, St. Augustine.

"The week before we opened": Dan Holiday, *Just Plane Dumb Luck* (self-published by Holiday, 2013), 37.

The menu at La Collage: ibid., 36.

"One day these kids arrived": ibid., 37.

One of the waitresses: Dan Holiday, interview, February 3, 2015.

Champion rarely spoke on stage: Johnson, *North Florida Folk Music*, 90.

Once while dining in a restaurant: Hookie Hamilton, interview by the author, March 3, 2014, St. Augustine.

Chapter 7

"Actually, we were friends who got married": Maggie Rogers, interview, March 8, 2015.

A prominent accomplishment: McGlane and McGlane, *Architecture*, 39.

"I always called him Gamble": Maggie Rogers, interview, March 8, 2015.

"His father was a very good musician": ibid.

Maggie said the cafe was named: ibid.

"There was a knight was drunk with wine": "The Baffled Knight," *Ballads and Lyrics of Love*, ed. Frank Sidgwick (New York: F. A. Stokes, 1908), 57.

Glore had earned a music scholarship: "Charles Scott Glore—76," Polk County, Obits, p. 3, http://fl-genweb.org/decole/Polk/obits/PcObits3.html.

If he were ever to succeed as a musician: Bruce McEwan, interview, February 16, 2014.

There was also Jimmie F. Rodgers: "Jimmie F. Rodgers, Biography," http://www.imdb.com/name/nm0734720/bio.

"The name Gamble Rogers had such a ring": Tony Perry, interview by the author, March 5, 2015, by phone.

"A fellow in the music department": ibid.

"Paul had such a unique character": John Perry, interview by the author, March 5, 2015, by phone.

"Are you really going to go": ibid.

"I just think Gamble knew": ibid.

Lewis, from Chicago: "Herschell Gordon Lewis: Biography," http://www.imdb.com/name/nm0504496/bio?ref_=nm_ov_bio_sm.

"Herschell Lewis made a bet with friends": Maggie Rogers, interview, March 8, 2015.

"Madmen Crazed for Carnage": *2,000 Maniacs* (1964) trailer, Daily Motion, http://www.dailymotion.com/video/x54s892.

"We had a station wagon": Maggie Rogers, interview, March 8, 2015.

"I think they just ran out of steam": ibid.

Chapter 8

"Serendipity always rewards the prepared": "Road Back to Russia, Paved with a Play," Katori Hall, *New York Times*, August 18, 2011.

"There's no doubt my brother would have been a very good architect": Jack Rogers, interview, June 6, 2014.

"It was a very forward-looking, humanistic design": ibid.

"When I was a young child": Lolly Rogers, interview by the author, December 29, 2014, Crescent Beach, FL.

"We all really loved Paul Champion": Chuck Rogers, interview by the author, March 31, 2105, St. Augustine.

"I was sort of a busy kid": ibid.

"In those early days": Maggie Rogers, interview, March 8, 2105.

"It was a stopping off point": ibid.

"The door was always open": Marc Eliot, *Death of a Rebel: A Biography of Phil Ochs* (New York: Franklin Watts, 1989), 55–56.

"Bob Dylan was there all the time": Maggie Rogers, interview, March 8, 2015.

"Gamble was very studied": ibid.

"It was a struggle": ibid.

"He even practiced scales": ibid.

Borrowing a quote: "Ignacy Jan Paderewski Quotes," IZQuotes, http://izquotes. com/author/ignacy-jan-paderewski.

Back home in Winter Park: Maggie Rogers, interview, March 8, 2015.

By 1966 Gamble made a decision: Jack Rogers, interview, June 6, 2014.

On the trip up to Boston: Tony Perry, interview, March 5, 2015.

The audition was held at the Bitter End: ibid.

"I had a pretty strong set prepared": ibid.

Not surprisingly, Gamble blew them away: ibid.

"We didn't have a lead guitar player": John Perry, interview, March 5, 2015.

Gamble and Tony were hired: ibid.

"Gamble never even went back to Florida:" Tony Perry, interview, March 5, 2015.

"That was the end of the Boston adventure": Maggie Rogers, interview, March 8, 2015.

"He wanted to tell me": Jack Rogers, interview, June 6, 2014.

"Oh my God": Tony Perry, interview, March 5, 2015.

"Well, it's a hard way to earn a living": Jack Rogers, interview, June 6, 2014.

Chapter 9

The singing ensemble got its start: "The Serendipity Singers: Colorado Music Hall of Fame Inductees," PopBopRockUntilUDrop, https://kimsloans. wordpress.com/colorado-local/colorado-1960s/colo-musicians-russo-tune/ serendipity-singers/.

Under the management of the folk impresario: Bruce Eder, "Serendipity Singers Biography," AllMusic, http://www.allmusic.com/artist/serendipity-singers -mn0000003224/biography.

The group was discouraged from playing the song: Hugh Boulware, "Serendipity's There Despite New Faces," *Chicago Tribune*, November 3, 1988, http://articles.chicagotribune.com/1988-11-03/features/8802120811_1_kingston-trio-serendipity-singers-music.

The other musical acts: *The Ed Sullivan Show*, season 17, episode 14, TV.com, http://www.tv.com/shows/the-ed-sullivan-show/december-27-1964-the-supremes-leslie-uggams-the-serendipity-singers-frank-gorshin-rip-taylor-106589/.

"It was a tough time": Maggie Rogers, interview, March 8, 2015.

"Gamble was not good with deadlines": Tony Perry, interview, March 5, 2015.

"We used to give him a call": John Perry, interview, March 5, 2015.

"He was so intelligent": ibid.

"Gamble was Gamble all the time": Tony Perry, interview, March 5, 2015.

For their appearance on the Ed Sullivan show: "Students and Adults Applaud Serendipity," *Freeport (IL) Journal Standard*, March 16, 1967.

"The Sullivan show was such a big deal": Tony Perry, interview, March 5, 2015.

Myron Cohen, the Borscht Belt comedian: ibid.

John Perry left the group: ibid.

"Gamble used that term of out modesty": ibid.

"His influence has never left us": ibid.

PART III. OKLAWAHA COUNTY LAISSEZ-FAIRE

Chapter 10

"Absorbed in the beauty": Jack Rogers, in "Gamble Rogers Tribute at the 1992 Florida Folk Festival," Florida Memory, https://www.floridamemory.com/items/show/237000.

"With its curved canopy": ibid.

But the work was not steady: Stiteler, "Gamble's Winning Bet," 12.

"Used to be the best trout fishing": Gamble Rogers, "Cape Canaveral Talking Blues," *Oklawaha County Laissez-Faire*.

"Disney World": Gamble Rogers, live performance, June 27, 1976, Jacksonville Civic Auditorium, concert tape from Larry Mangum.

Chapter 11

Elizabeth Seneff was born: "Replacing Judy Henske: Was Liz Seneff Enough?" *Ill Folks*, May 19, 2012, http://illfolks.blogspot.com/2012/05/replacing-judy-henske-was-liz-seneff.html.

As a solo performer in New York: Bob Patterson, interview by the author, August 27, 2014, Crescent Beach, FL.

Billing itself as "Florida's Most Unique Coffee House": Lee Zimmerman, "The Flick: Miami's Legendary Music Club and Coffeehouse Celebrates Its 50th Anniversary," *Miami New Times*, March 11, 2014, http://www.miaminewtimes.com/music/the-flick-miamis-legendary-music-club-and-coffeehouse-celebrates-its-50th-anniversary-6449006.

"A booking at the Flick": Michael Peter Smith, interview by the author, January 19, 2015, by phone.

"In the early '60s": ibid.

"He could have walked in straight": ibid.

"Humor had to be added": ibid.

"His wife, Elfrieda": Gamble Rogers, 1971, *Tales from the Flick*, #2. https://www.youtube.com/watch?v=5ENVA88QfSM.

"He was a southern gentleman": Michael Peter Smith, interview, January 19, 2015.

"I recently saw a photo of Liz": ibid.

Chapter 12

"What a funky place the Tradewinds is": Gamble Rogers, Jacksonville Civic Auditorium, June 27, 1976, recording from Larry Mangum.

Less than twenty-four hours earlier: Bob Patterson, interview, August 27, 2014.

Billed as "the Oldest Lounge": Tradewinds Lounge, http://tradewindslounge.com/about/.

"The Tradewinds was an amazing place": Bob Patterson, interview, August 27, 2014.

"He would arrive in a hearse": ibid.

"From the street outside": ibid.

"We were both kind of the black sheep": ibid.

"Saturday nights at the Tradewinds": ibid.

"There would be nights": ibid.

"There would be tables": ibid.

"The amazing thing about Gamble": ibid.

"Now I could tell by the clothes he was wearing": Gamble Rogers, "The Dekalb County Deputy Sheriff," *Lord Gives Me Grace*.

"I'll tell you after twenty years": Gamble Rogers, "Liars Workshop Performing at the 1987 Florida Folk Festival," May 22, 1987, Florida Memory, https://www.floridamemory.com/items/show/237812

"This is the last guitar": Gamble Rogers, "Hard Times Don't Scare Me None," *Sorry Is as Sorry Does*.

"He was pretty drunk": Bruce McEwan, interview, February 16, 2014.

"It wasn't the kind of place": Jack Rogers, interview, June 6, 2014.

"On Palm Sunday": Jim Carrick, interview, December 12, 2013.

"Whenever Gamble was in town": Charley Simmons, interview by the author, April 8, 2014, St. Augustine.

"A typical Tradewinds Saturday night": Gamble Rogers, Jacksonville Civic Auditorium, June 27, 1976.

"A skull orchard": Gamble Rogers, "The Terminal Tavern," *Oklawaha County Laissez-Faire*.

Chapter 13

"For the Ancient City": Gamble Rogers, introduction to "Doris," *Lord Gives Me Grace.*

As a child, Gamble's mother: Lyn Rogers Lacey, interview, November 18, 2014.

"I remember asking him once": ibid.

"It's not that I hate Disney World": ibid.

"There was an almost mystical atmosphere": Jim Carrick, interview, December 12, 2013.

"I was just blown away": ibid.

"I followed him everywhere": ibid.

"He was an example of someone who lived in the truth": ibid.

"You couldn't go over sixty miles per hour": ibid.

"Charlie Robertson is God's personal songwriter": Gamble Rogers, quoted at Charlie Robertson's Real website, http://www.charlierobertsonmusic.com.

"That's one of the things you long for": Charlie Robertson, interview by the author, February 5, 2014, St. Augustine.

"I had written a few songs myself": ibid.

"It was typical of the kind of stuff he wrote then": ibid.

"Oh, the green Ohio River": Gamble Rogers, "The Girl from Stoney Lonesome," *Good Causes,* Oklawaha Records, Steady Arm Music (BMI), 2003 and 2016.

"That's where he worked out all of his stories": Charlie Robertson, interview, February 5, 2014.

"Gamble inserted himself": ibid.

"I didn't know I was this good": ibid.

Robertson was among those: ibid.

"That was an interesting relationship": ibid.

"You have to realize": Bob Patterson, interview, August 27, 2014.

"What I learned is that Gamble": Charlie Robertson, interview, February 5, 2014.

"As accomplished as he was": ibid.

"It was as if they'd put him through": ibid.

"We walked past this terrible-looking Trailways": ibid.

Chapter 14

"It was exactly twenty years ago": Gamble Rogers, introduction to "Orange Blossom Special," with Will McLean, May 25, 1982, Florida Folk Festival, Florida Memory, https://www.floridamemory.com/audio/folk.php#05.

Born in Chipley: Johnson, *North Florida Folk Music,* 55.

Legend has it: ibid., 57.

When he returned to Florida: ibid.

A man of few possessions: ibid., 59.

"So I called Gamble": Paul Berger, interview by the author, April 9, 2014, St. Augustine.

"Well, you know Will's a good friend": ibid.

"Will's stories were magical": Bob Patterson, interview, August 27, 2014.

"Oh, Gamble I ain't nothin'": Jim Carrick, live performance, April 30, 2015, Mudville Listening Room, Jacksonville, FL, author's notes.

"Will McClean knew": Gamble Rogers, eulogy for Will McLean, January 1990, Thomas Center, Gainesville, recorded by Donna Green-Townsend, http://donnagreentownsend.com/will-mclean/#.WKXC1RBQo7A.

"You can only play basketball for so long": Dale Crider, interview by the author, November 8, 2015, Beluthahatchee Park, St. Johns County, FL.

"Oh, bring him along": ibid.

"We rapped and rapped": ibid.

"Don't leave the kids with a picker": Larry Mangum and the Cowboy Orchestra, "Ballad of Dale and Gamble," Mangum Music, 2008.

"We as human beings": Bob Patterson, interview, August 27, 2014.

Chapter 15

The back seat was often littered: Bob Patterson, interview, August 27, 2014.

"Those first long trips": ibid.

"I seem to be on the verge of commercial success": Gamble Rogers, quoted in Evelyn August, "Singer Prefers Guitar to Using Slide Rule," Associated Press, reprint, *Evening Standard* (Uniontown, PA), June 6, 1974.

Chuck Glaser was predicting big things for Gamble: Evelyn August, "Singer Prefers Guitar."

"The emotion of that music spoke to me": Charles Steadham, interview by the author, August 1, 2015, St. Augustine.

He was motivated in part: ibid.

"It was a really a novelty": ibid.

"I couldn't find an honest agent to represent us": ibid.

"The drummer will run off": ibid.

"He told me about this": ibid.

"Gamble had them in the palm of his hand": ibid.

"You couldn't meet Gamble": ibid.

"Chuck had his hands full": ibid.

"I knew immediately if Gamble told me something": ibid.

"As much as he understood the business side": ibid.

"We live in a consumer economy": Gamble Rogers, "Cape Canaveral Talking Blues," *Oklawaha County Laissez-Faire*.

Another challenge: Charles Steadham, interview, August 1, 2015.

The audition was arranged by Jim Stafford: Jim Stafford, interview by the author, February 27, 2017, by phone.

"We played a lot of the same places": ibid.

"One of the reasons": ibid.

"With Tommy, you needed to really score": ibid.

"They would welcome his level of artistry": Charles Steadham, interview, August 1, 2015.

"He knew I wouldn't deliberately put him": ibid.

"They were throwing a soiree": ibid.

"I had seen this man staring at Gamble": Charles Steadham, interview by the author, December 6, 2015, St. Augustine.

"He didn't want or need to hear": ibid.

Chapter 16

Nancy Lee was born in Texas: Nancy Rogers, interview by Paul Linser, *Gamble Gazette* (Fall 2001).

She spent time at a boarding school: Lory Pounder, "Family and Friends Remember Nancy Rogers," *St. Augustine Record*, January 3, 2005.

"That's how it all started with Nancy": Bob Patterson, interview, August 27, 2014.

"In a lot of ways she seemed Janis Joplin-like": Sid Ansbacher, interview by the author, October 1, 2013, Jacksonville, FL.

"Pretty much everything happened at the Tradewinds": Bob Patterson, interview, August 27, 2014.

Other accounts have her introducing herself: Nancy Rogers, interview by Paul Linser, *Gamble Gazette*, Fall 2001.

"She always said it was his voice": Neely Ann Miller, interview by the author, May 4, 2016, St. Augustine.

"Nancy was beautiful": Bob Patterson, interview, August 27, 2014.

"I told her I didn't know her": Hookie Hamilton, interview by the author, March 3, 2014, St. Augustine.

"Gamble had this ancient bike:" Sid Ansbacher, interview, October 1, 2013.

"Nancy wouldn't pull any punches": Bob Patterson, interview August 27, 2014.

"Dear Nancy": Gamble Rogers to Nancy (Lee) Frost, June 8, 1977.

They had been housesitting: "Gamble Rogers Drowns," *St. Augustine Record*, October 11, 1991.

"I don't think another marriage": Bob Patterson, interview, August 27, 2014.

Vows: obtained from Neely Ann Miller and used with permission.

"There was a lot of family stuff going on": Bob Patterson, interview, August 27, 2014.

"He had that gift": Lyn Rogers Lacey, interview, November 18, 2014.

"He was a magnificent father": Stephanie Frost, interview by the author, December 27, 2016, St. Augustine.

"If I was ever going through anything": Lyn Rogers Lacey, interview, November 18, 2014.

"That's how he was with all of us,": ibid.

As a young adult, Lyn was teaching: ibid.

"Well, what you have to remember": ibid.

"He had this way of looking": ibid.

"If I could play anywhere:" ibid.

"I just swooned": ibid.

"I was a really lucky kid:" Lolly Rogers, interview, December 29, 2014.

Stephanie recalled how on special holidays: Stephanie Frost, interview, December 27, 2016.

"He would take his binder checkbook": ibid.

"He was being truthful": Lyn Rogers Lacey interview, November 18, 2014.

Chapter 17

"The stories I tell are all true": Gamble Rogers, quoted in "Biography: James Gamble Rogers IV," Gamble Rogers Memorial Foundation, http://gamblerogers. org/life/.

"They were the very same characters": Jim Carrick, interview, December 12, 2013.

"Everybody in town knows what everybody else is doing": Gamble Rogers, "Troubadour Emeritus," © Steady Arm Music (BMI), at Gamble Rogers Memorial Foundation, GambleRogers.com.

Snipes Ford served as the mythical county seat: ibid.

"It's not what you are thinking": ibid.

In addition to the rural alchemists: *Gamble Rogers Home Grown Philosophy* Part One DVD, originally recorded 1984, released by Gamble Rogers Memorial Foundation 2010, Oklawaha Records.

"Experience is what you get": James Gamble Rogers IV, *Oklawaha County Doctrines of Citizenship*.

"Dear people": Gamble Rogers, "Still Bill's Blind Walk," *Sorry Is as Sorry Does.*

"D-A-W-G": Gamble Rogers, "Dogs and Dawgs," *Oklawaha County Laissez-Faire.*

Gamble clearly preferred "dawgs": Bob Patterson interview, August 27, 2014.

"The way Gamble would walk": ibid.

"Some people may have used these words": Lyn Rogers Lacey, interview, November 18, 2014.

In Keillor's Lake Wobegon: Garrison Keillor, introduction to *Prairie Home Companion* radio program.

"They're so primitive in Bean Creek": Gamble Rogers, "Bean Creek Alphabet," *Sorry Is as Sorry Does.*

"My stories, for instance": Gamble Rogers, quoted in Stiteler, "Gamble's Winning Bet," 13–14.

"His real art": Jim Carrick, interview, December 12, 2013.

"He got to a point": ibid.

"He was a remarkable musician": James Lee Stanley, interview by the author, April 2014, by phone.

Chapter 18

"The Lord gives me grace": Gamble Rogers, "Habersham County Mephistopheles," *Lord Gives Me Grace.*

"Every song was literature": Charles Steadham, interview, August 1, 2015.

"Doris moved": Gamble Rogers, introduction to "Doris," *Lord Gives Me Grace.*

"This could have easily been": Charlie Robertson, quoted in Michael Reynolds, "Gamble Rogers, the Architecture Student Who Became a Storyteller," *Folio Weekly*, October 19, 1993, 11.

"And I pity the poor Yankee bastards", Gamble Rogers, "Kennesaw Line," by Don Dunaway, *Lord Gives Me Grace*.

"Here's one of those songs my Daddy used to sing": Gamble Rogers, introduction to "Two Little Boys," *Oklawaha County Laissez-Faire*.

"In the real world": Gamble Rogers, in *Gamble Rogers: Songs and Stories*, ed. Charles V. Steadham Jr. and Harold Fethe (Gainesville, FL, Steady Arm Music, 2006), 41.

"It was a big deal to me": Michael Peter Smith, interview, January 19, 2015.

"The songs that he wrote": ibid.

"He translated it for people": ibid.

"Let's say": ibid.

"He told me they would love me": ibid.

"What I saw": ibid.

"I thought Gamble's version was the more accurate one": ibid.

"Let us go to the banks of the ocean": Michael Peter Smith, "The Dutchman," *Juarez*, Bird Avenue (ASCAP), 1970.

"What he did with 'The Dutchman'": Michael Peter Smith, interview, January 19, 2015.

"Take it easy, boy": Gamble Rogers, performance at Marjorie Kinnan Rawlings State Historic Site, 50th anniversary of *The Yearling*, 1988, on YouTube, https://m.youtube.com/watch?v=cQrXhnZFZis.

Chapter 19

"I ain't nothing but a whiskey salesman": Frank Thomas, interview, May 7, 2014.

"He did a lot of Harry Chapin music": Mike Schneider, interview by the author, January 26, 2016, Jacksonville, FL.

"We took the concept of the listening room literally": ibid.

"In the beginning there was a learning curve": ibid.

"A lot of the performers we booked": ibid.

"They weren't just coming for an office party": ibid.

"He never seemed to have an off night": ibid.

"He was never real comfortable": ibid.

"You're not going to pay me": ibid.

"He cared about the owners": Lyn Rogers Lacey, interview, November 18, 2014.

MacDonald remembered a particular gig: Rod MacDonald, interview by the author, March 29, 2016, by phone.

"I think his back had been bothering him": ibid.

Mangum, who expected a crowd of about two thousand: Larry Mangum, interview by the author, June 6, 2014, Jacksonville, FL.

"I'm just guessing": ibid.

"It's one of the best concerts": ibid.

"I remember the bus driving away": ibid.

Buffett dedicated his 1994 *Fruitcakes* CD: Jimmy Buffet, *Fruitcakes*, notes, March 16, 1994.

"They still love you": Jimmy Buffett, *A Pirate Looks at Fifty* (New York: Ballantine Books, 1998), 250.

"I love the scale of what I'm doing": Lyn Rogers Lacey, interview, November 18, 2014.

Gamble saw the music business: ibid.

Chapter 20

"Sometimes the best stories are lies": Gamble Rogers, quoted in "Reflections of a Wandering Storyteller," Associated Press, reprint, *Indiana Evening Gazette*, June 1, 1981.

The inaugural festival was deemed a huge success: "One of America's Oldest and Largest Folk Festivals," Florida State Parks, https://www.floridastateparks.org/folkfest/history.

A little-known Gamble Rogers: "Sunday Performances at the 1963 Florida Folk Festival," May 5, 1963, Florida Memory, https://www.floridamemory.com/items/show/239450.

"A lot of people say White Springs": Dennis Devine, "Liars Workshop," Florida Memory, https://www.floridamemory.com/items/show/237812.

"I knew if he could play anything like Paul Champion": Frank Thomas, interview, May 7, 2014.

"I ain't nothing extree": ibid.

"He was a great musician": ibid.

"Listen Frank, we are all the adopted children": ibid.

Disque was a design professor: Gamble Rogers, "Liars Workshop," Florida Memory, https://www.floridamemory.com/items/show/237812.

"That was some of the best advice": ibid.

Gamble also spoke of his other great influence: ibid.

"So if anybody wants to tell stories": ibid.

"Every time my mother hears": ibid.

"A lie is not necessarily a prevarication": ibid.

He used none other than "Honest Abe": ibid.

"And so it is, with the retelling": ibid.

The short summary of the performance: Gamble Rogers, "Nine Pound Hammer," *Oklawaha County Laissez-Faire*.

"The fact that the bull ran up the fence": Florida Memory, https://www.floridamemory.com/items/show/237812.

"It was always my blessing": ibid.

"The trick to satire or poking fun": ibid.

Chapter 21

"He slept only fours hours a night": Jim Carrick, interview, December 12, 2013.
"Gamble hated what was being done to the Ocklawaha": Bob Patterson, interview, August 27, 2014.
"He liked how they planned to buy": ibid.
Legend has it: Bruce McEwan, interview, February 16, 2014.
Gamble joked: ibid.
"Gamble came up close": Pete Seeger, "Pete Seeger Remembering Gamble Rogers," on YouTube, https://www.youtube.com/watch?v=DiRyNaxMo_s.
Gamble also sought out the company: Bob Patterson, interview, August 2014.
Gamble appears in the film: *Heartworn Highways,* 1976, directed and written by James Szalapski.
"When he'd finish": Rod MacDonald, interview, March 29, 2016.
"The musical narrative": Gamble Rogers to Nancy (Lee) Frost, June 8, 1977.
"He had charisma": David Dowling, interview by the author, May 16, 2016, St. Augustine.
"They gave him some blood": ibid.
"It goes back to the old adage": ibid.
"Paul is the only person I know": Jim Carrick, interview, December 12, 2013.
"It wasn't that Paul didn't have any business sense": David Dowling, interview, May 16, 2016.
Before moving to Florida Berger worked: Paul Berger, interview, April 9, 2014.
Berger had somehow managed: ibid.
On one occasion, Dowling and a few others: David Dowling, interview, May 16, 2016.
The judge then paused for a moment: ibid.

Chapter 22

"His actions, the way he lived his life": Sam Pacetti, interview by the author, February 24, 2016, St. Augustine.
"I had strategically positioned myself": Sam Pacetti, interview by the author, October 17, 2013, St. Augustine.
"He asked if I would be interested in getting together": ibid.
"I watched my dad": ibid.
"It was like a holy grail": ibid.
"Gamble was aware there were certain areas": ibid.
"Well, you owe me forty dollars": Bob Parsons, interview by the author, November 21, 2013, St. Augustine.
"We'd be working on something and Gamble would call us": Billy Qualls, interview by the author, November 21, 2103, St. Augustine.
"I think he was just trying to create a big community": Bob Parsons, interview, November 21, 2013.
"Gamble was like a second dad": ibid.

"All my summer days": Neely Ann Miller, unpublished essay.

Lis heard about Gamble: Lis Williamson, interview by the author, June 14, 2014, Keystone Heights, FL.

"She had all these hot guitar licks": ibid.

"One day we looked out our window": Lon Williamson, interview by the author, June 14, 2014, Keystone Heights, FL.

"He would just sketch out these ideas": ibid.

"His kindness to others": Lis Williamson, interview, June 14, 2014.

"It's good for me": Lon Williamson, interview, June 14, 2014.

"I told Gamble slow it down": ibid.

Part IV. Troubadour Emeritus

Chapter 23

He had officially retired: Jack Rogers, interview, June 6, 2014.

Occasionally they attended: ibid.

"When he was forty-three years of age": Gamble Rogers, "My Father Was a Voyager," 1990, in *A Good Man: Fathers and Sons in Poetry and Prose*, ed. Irv Broughton (New York: Fawcett Columbine, 1993) 27.

Chapter 24

"We all knew someday": Bob Patterson, interview, August 27, 2014.

Gamble helped spearhead fund-raising: Dean Johnson, "Orlando Bluegrass Musician Needs Heart Transplant," *Orlando Sentinel*, February 8, 1986, articles.orlandosentinel.com.

"He went about organizing": Jim Carrick, interview, December 12, 2013.

"It is my suspicion": Sam Pacetti, interview, October 17, 2013.

"He would call and say": ibid.

"Gamble had this look": ibid.

"McEwan, you are going to die an early death": Bruce McEwan, interview, February 16, 2014.

"It had been tough": Lyn Rogers Lacey, interview, November 18, 2014.

Late in the summer of 1991: ibid.

"He couldn't hold her enough": ibid.

"I walked to the end of the sidewalk": ibid.

"It was God's way of preparing me": ibid.

"So much to do . . . no time left": Stephanie Frost, interview, December 27, 2016.

Chapter 25

"They were trying to get Gamble to come down": Frank Thomas interview, May 7, 2014.

"If there was one date in my life": Charles Steadham, interview, December 6, 2015.

"There's one date in my career": ibid.

"Gamble was involved": Sid Ansbacher, interview, October 1, 2013.

"He had an amazing library": ibid.

Following the morning bike ride: ibid.

Moments earlier a terrified teenager: ibid.

Park Ranger Chuck McIntire: ibid.

"At one point, he encountered Gamble": Dana Treen, "Gamble Rogers Drowns Trying to Save Man," *Florida Times-Union*, October 12, 1991.

"She was very shaken and weakened": Sid Ansbacher, interview, October 1, 2013.

"There was Gamble": ibid.

"The belly was bloated": ibid.

A rescue team: Treen, "Gamble Rogers Drowns."

It was not the first time: Bob Patterson, interview, August 27, 2014.

"Gamble could not turn his head": Sam Pacetti, interview, October 17, 2013.

"He had no choice": Jim Carrick, interview, December 12, 2013.

"He was a very gentle soul": Sid Ansbacher, interview, October 1, 2013.

"Going back to that day": ibid.

"I'm just relieved it was him before me": Stephanie Frost, interview, December 27, 2016.

Chapter 26

"Voyager upon Life's Sea": Sarah T. Bolton, *Life and Poems of Sarah T. Bolton* (Indianapolis, IN: Fred L. Horton, 1880), digital edition, 277, Archive.org.

"It's like Where were you": Bob Patterson, interview, August 27, 2014.

With legal assistance from others: Stephanie Frost, interview, December 27, 2016.

"It was then I realized the magnitude": Sid Ansbacher, interview, October 1, 2013.

"I just went in the back": Lolly Rogers, interview, December 2014.

"I sequestered myself": Sam Pacetti, interview, October 17, 2013.

A few blocks away: Jim Carrick, interview, December 12, 2013.

"I was devastated": Charles Steadham, interview, December 6, 2015.

"I find it easier": ibid.

"In the dream": Jim Carrick, interview, December 12, 2013.

Chapter 27

Lopez recalled a time: Harvey Lopez, interview by the author, July 16, 2016.

It set in motion: ibid.

"When we first got started": ibid.

Meanwhile, to accommodate a viewing: Stephanie Frost, interview, December 27, 2016.

"It is not something you want to get good at": ibid.

The music playing in the truck's cabin: Harvey Lopez, interview, July 16, 2016.

"You have to have a paddle": ibid.

"One more white shirt": Gamble Rogers, "Sketches of Nostalgia," *Warm Way Home.*

"Dear Grandpa": Neely Ann Miller, from the collection of Nancy Rogers.

The Tradewinds Tropical Lounge ran ads: *First Coast Entertainer,* October 19, 1991.
"Gamble was my best friend": Lyn Rogers Lacey, interview, November 18, 2014.
"Daddy was playing at the club": ibid.
"Daddy apparently made arrangements": ibid.
"He said he never met him": Charles Steadham, interview, December 6, 2015.

Chapter 28

"Gamble Rogers was a troubadour": Nancy Lee Rogers to Florida Arts Council, October 20, 1993.
Bob Parsons, his neighbor and friend: Bob Parsons, interview, November 21, 2013.
Jim Carrick recalled a similar emotion: Jim Carrick, interview, December 12, 2013.
"It came sweeping in from all sides": Nancy Rogers to "Dear Friends," November 1991.
"He loved the land": ibid.
WHEREAS, James Gamble IV: Laws of Florida, Chapter 92-11, edocs.dlis.state. fl.us/fldocs/leg/actsflorida/1992/1992v1Pt2.pdf.
The park consistently boasts: Barbara Roberts, park manager, interview by the author, November 7, 2013.
The *St. Augustine Record* newspaper: "Erase Gamble Rogers' Legacy?" editorial, *St. Augustine Record*, November 7, 2013.
Her dream was to establish a real Oklawaha County: Nancy Rogers to "Dear Friends," November 1991.

Chapter 29

The Gamble Rogers Memorial Foundation was established: Articles of Incorporation, Gamble Rogers Memorial Foundation.
At the time of his death: Bill DeYoung, "Remembering Gamble" *Gainesville Sun,* October 11, 1994.
For his part: ibid.
"Since Gamble's death": ibid.
"It's gone on too long": ibid.
Steadham meanwhile focused: Charles Steadham, interview, December 6, 2015.
"Gamble Rogers is a Florida legend": Nancy Lee Rogers to Florida Arts Council, October 20, 1993.
"I was privileged": Stetson Kennedy to Florida Arts Council, Division of Cultural Affairs, October 23, 1993.
"I personally know of no one": Jimmy Buffett to Florida Artists Hall of Fame, Division of Cultural Affairs, May 25, 1995.

Chapter 30

The Gamble Rogers Folk Festival: Meredith Ridenour, "Remembering Gamble Rogers," *St. Augustine Record,* April 30, 2004, http://staugustine.com/stories/043004/com_2274046.shtml#.WK7wSBBQo7A.

At the urging of Dan Downs: ibid.

"Gamble Rogers was an entertainer": Gamble Rogers Folk Festival Souvenir Program, 1996, p. 3.

Lagasse never met Gamble: CD booklet, *Oklawaha County Jamboree*, Gatorbone Records, 2014, p. 7.

"I wanted to make a CD": ibid., 8.

She was embroiled: Bob Patterson, interview, August 27, 2014.

The disease ravaged: Lory Pounder, "Family and Friends Remember Nancy Rogers as a Free Spirit," *St. Augustine Record*, January 3, 2005.

"I'm not getting any younger": Bob Patterson, interview, August 27, 2014.

Jim Carrick recalled: Jim Carrick, interview by the author, July 16, 2016.

"We had already made our minds up": ibid.

"He probably wouldn't want a book": Lyn Rogers Lacey, interview, November 18, 2014.

Epilogue

"Gamble was as close to perfect": Michael Peter Smith, Lohman Auditorium, Marineland, FL, August 24, 2013, author's notes.

"Whole lot of country, whole lot of blues": Michael Peter Smith, "Gamble's Guitar," Bird Avenue (ASCAP).

"It's tempting": Lyn Rogers Lacey, interview, November 18, 2014.

"He's about as close as you get": Jim Stafford, interview, February 27, 2017.

"His music brought me pleasure": email to Charles Steadham, April 9, 2003.

"All of his stories and songs": Lolly Rogers, interview, December 29, 2014.

"Gamble Rogers on occasion ate": P. S. Beresh, letter to the editor, *St. Augustine Record*, November 4, 1993.

"He was intelligent enough to know": Sam Pacetti, interview, October 17, 2013.

The electric bill from Florida Power and Light: Neely Ann Miller, email to the author, January 4, 2017.

"I really didn't know that guy": ibid.

"All accolades": ibid.

"God bless old friends that have gone before": Michael Peter Smith, "Gamble's Guitar."

Index

Guthrie, Arlo, 181
Guthrie, Woody, 141
Gypsy Cab Company, 35

Haggard, Merle, 144
Hall, John "Sleepy," 13
Hamilton, Hookie, 108
Harris, Joel Chandler, 14
Hatchett Creek Music Festival, 63
Hatsell, Sharon, 180
Heartworn Highways (film), 141–42
Hell's Belles, 1
Hemingway, Ernest, 5, 82, 177
Henry, Red, 148
Herndon, William, 137
Holiday, Dan, 40–41
"Home Grown Lucifer (Habersham County Mephistopheles)" (song), 123
"Honeycomb" (song), 44
"The Honeydipper" (song), 126
Hootenanny (television show), 53
"House of the Rising Sun" (song), 49

Ingram, Bob, 78

Jenkins, Tom, 165
Jennings, Waylon, 100, 102
J. Geils Band, 130
Johnson, Robert, 83
Jones, Agamemnon, 1, 2, 6, 36, 117, 183
Jonesboro Storytelling Festival, 140
"July You're a Woman" (song), 124
Just Plane Dumb Luck (Holiday), 41

Keillor, Garrison, 119–20
Kennedy, Stetson, 140–41, 177–78
"Kennesaw Line" (song), 35, 124
Kickasola, Ron, 78
King, Martin Luther, Jr., 41
Kinsey, Brad, 167–68
Knowles Avenue house, 48
Kristofferson, Kris, 100

Lacey, Lyn Rogers: birth, 48, 58; family photograph, 61; Gamble's availability as a father, 111–12, 114–15; Gamble's Carnegie Hall performance, 113; Gamble's meeting with William Faulkner, 36; Gamble's opinion of Disney World, 89; Gamble's solo music career, 129, 131–32; Gamble's storytelling, 119; memorials and tributes to Gamble, 169–70, 183, 186; Nacoochee Valley family farm, 28–31; performing with Gamble, 112–13; premonitions of Gamble's death, 157–58
Lacey, Meghan, 157, 181
Lagasse, Mike, 181
"The Last Troubadour" (song), 130, 181, 195–96
Le Collage cafe, 40–41
Lee, Peggy, 2
Leonard, Toni, 82
Leonard, Walter "Duke," 82
Lewis, Herschell Gordon, 45
Liars Workshop, 135–38
Lincoln, Abraham, 135, 136–37
Linser, Paul, 181
Log Cabin Boys, 40
"Long Legged Women" (song), 123
Lopez, Harvey, 167–68
Lyndell, Linda, 101

MacDonald, Rod, 129–30, 141–42
Madden, Edward, 124
Madden, John, 142
Magnolia Drive home, 66, 90, 110, 145, 146–50, 156, 158, 165, 188
"Mama Blue" (song), 123
Mangum, Larry, 130, 181
Martin, Vince, 78
Mason, Connie, 45
"The Masterbuilders" (song), 50, 134
Masters, Edgar Lee, 120
McCartney, Paul, 144
McEwan, Bruce: death of, 182; friendship with Gamble, 19–20, 21, 23, 58, 85, 140, 157; Gamble's legacy, 171, 177, 186
McEwan, M.L., 140
McIntire, Chuck, 161
McLean, Will: Cassadaga Stories, 92; death of, 135, 155, 156; Florida Folk Festival, 68, 134; folk music revival, 6, 95–96; friendship with Gamble, 44, 89, 93, 94, 95–97, 148; Tradewinds Tropical Lounge, 81
Midnight Sons, 12–13
Miller, Neely Ann, 69, 108, 148, 168–69, 182, 188
Milne, Caroline, 35
Milne, Jack, 35

BRUCE HOROVITZ is an award-winning journalist and an entrepreneur with extensive experience in the nonprofit and business communities. He is a graduate of Boston University's School of Public Communication. This is his first book. He lives with his family in Jacksonville, Florida, where he serves on several nonprofit boards while pursuing his musical interests by playing in two bands.